MODERN MILITARY AIRCRAFT

Dr. Thomas Bruce

MODERN MILITARY AIRCRAFT

by Dr. Thomas Bruce

Copyright © 2023 by the author

All rights reserved.

TABLE OF CONTENTS

Introduction

Modern Fighter Aircraft

Modern Strategic Bombers

Modern Attack Helicopter

Air-Launched Weapons

Anti-Aircraft / Anti-Missile Systems

Unmanned Aerial Systems

Conclusions

INTRODUCTION

Since their introduction, aircraft have become a key aspect of any conflict between nations. Aircraft are used to provide reconnaissance, transportation, airborne radar, electronic jamming, air-to-air combat and of course ground attack. Ground attack is performed by a range of aircraft types encompassing strategic (bombers), tactical bombers (fighter-bombers) and helicopters. Ground attack weapons launched from these aircraft include guided and unguided bombs, rockets, guided missiles, ballistic missiles, cruise missiles and cannon fire. Ground targets include enemy AFV's, artillery positions, infantry units, structures associated with command and control, radar facilities, ground-based weapons launch facilities, military storage locations as well as other targets deemed of strategic or tactical value, including civil infrastructure.

Prior to the development of missiles, fighter aircraft were classified by names such as heavy fighters, interceptors, escort fighters, night-fighters and fighter-bombers, with a variety of designs reflecting the wide range of specialized roles. With the development of guided missiles, fighter aircraft design diverged between interceptors optimized to attack in the 'beyond visual range' (BVR) regime and dog-fighters optimized to fight in the 'within visual range' (WVR) regime. The small agile dog-fighters were armed with cannon and short-range missiles, but were unable to carry heavy missile payloads. The large cumbersome interceptors by contrast, which relied upon the launching of long range missiles to destroy their targets, lacked the ability to defend themselves in a close-in engagement. Early long-range missiles proved unreliable at consistently hitting their targets, especially the agile dog-fighters, and therefore the poorly maneuvering interceptors often found themselves in close combat situations for which they were ill suited.

The solution was to fuse the two fighter jet aircraft concepts into one - the Air Superiority Fighter. These aircraft could launch missiles at targets over long distances as well as engage other aircraft at close-range in tight maneuvering aerial combat. Early air superiority fighters included the American F-15 Eagle and the Russian Su-27 Flanker. In time these aircraft were modified so that they could also perform ground-attack missions. The new philosophy became to design a single aircraft able to perform all fighter aircraft roles, known as a Multirole Fighter. This approach avoided the expense associated with designing and operating multiple aircraft platforms. Multirole fighters are able operate in an air superiority role, engage in high maneuverability dog-fights and effectively strike ground targets.

Multirole 4th generation fighters are large and powerful enough to carry a heavy payload while enhanced maneuverability was achieved by relaxing their static stability. Relaxed Static Stability (RSS) causes aircraft flight path deviations to be exaggerated rather than to be resisted, as is typical for older fighters and modern transportation aircraft. The result in that aircraft with RSS are far more responsive to pilot inputs. Lack of stability increases maneuverability but risks loss of control of the aircraft. Therefore 4th generation fighters utilize fly-by-wire (FBW) digital flight controls. With FBW the pilot's controls are used to indicate how the pilot wants the aircraft to maneuver. Based on the pilots input the actual changes to the flight surfaces required to produce that maneuver is calculated and implemented by the flight control computer. Aircraft sensors take thousands of measurements per second and the on-board computer makes automated corrections to maintain stable flight.

The initial 4th generation aircraft however were understandably expensive compared to their predecessors. This high cost resulted in Airforce's operating far fewer aircraft than had previously been the case. The cost to both procure and operate such aircraft only continued to spiral upward as the aircraft were upgraded over the last 30 years with ever more advanced avionics, sensors, missile warning systems, active electronic scanned array (AESA) radar, digital avionic buses, high capacity data-links and infrared search and track (IRST) capabilities. Upgraded versions of these platforms, such as the F-15E Strike Eagle, F/A-18E/F Super Hornet and the Su-35 Flanker-E, are often referred to as 4.5 generation or 4+ generation aircraft.

Modern aircraft designs that have only recently emerged are referred to as 5th generation aircraft. The definition of what a 5th generation aircraft is has not yet been universally agreed upon. In general such aircraft typically possess some level of stealth, in which their radar cross-section (RCS) is reduced. Stealth characteristics are achieved through careful design of aircraft surfaces and concealment of weapons within internal weapons bays. Additionally novel composite materials and radar absorbing coating are employed. Stealth does not imply aircraft 'invisibility', but rather that the aircraft is more challenging to detect and specifically to accurately track – a necessary aspect of being able to engage an aircraft with air defense missiles.

Other common capabilities found on 5th Generation aircraft are thrust vectoring, supercruise, off-bore sight aiming and sensor fusion. Thrust vectoring increases maneuverability by redirecting the jet exhaust using flexible exhaust nozzles. While supercruise is the ability to achieve and maintain supersonic speeds without using afterburners, significantly reducing overall fuel consumption. Off-bore sight aiming involves firing missiles at targets that are not in line with the direction of the aircrafts travel and is accomplished by integrating the targeting display directly into the pilot's helmet. And networked sensor data fusion involves having the on-board computers handle most of the analysis of the data obtained by the aircraft's various sensors.

Multirole aircraft prior to 5th generation fighters typically came in two configurations; a single seat aircraft focused on air combat and a two seat aircraft with a focus on ground attack. This was because the effort to analyze the complex plethora of sensor data associated with ground attack missions was a burden on the pilot, who had to concentrate on flying the high performance fighter. Therefore a Weapons Systems Officer (WSO) was introduced into the second seat to focus on processing the sensor data and coordinating weapons aiming and launch. With the introduction of networked sensor data fusion this role became performed by the Flight Control System computer, removing the need for the WSO. Therefore 5th generation aircraft require only the single seat for the lone pilot, who with the assistance of the aircraft computer is able to execute complex ground attack missions on their own.

Sensor fusion also permits the sharing of data between the various airborne platforms in flight, as well as between aircraft and ground control systems. This capability provides the pilot of each aircraft with an unprecedented level of 3D long range situational awareness. Critically this enhanced awareness of the surrounding battlespace can provide the pilot the advantage of detecting their opponent first - and in aerial combat, the first to shoot typically wins. Operating through network-centric co-operation, the sharing of data between aircraft also permits the handing off of targets. A pilot who detects a target but is unable to engage it can simply assign the target to another more favorability positioned aircraft, ensuring that no opportunities are lost. Some of these advanced features of 5th generation fighters are also already available in a number of the 4.5 generation aircraft. We will review the most relevant 4.5 generation aircraft of the major world powers first, and then consider the 5th generation fighters.

In this book we discuss the dominant modern military combat aircraft used throughout the world, including fighter aircraft, strategic bombers and attack helicopter. The aircraft are grouped by the nation that developed them. We also review the predominantly employed modern weapon systems deployed by these aircraft, including guided bombs, guided missiles and cruise missiles. Modern weapon systems used to counter both aircraft (anti-aircraft systems) and additionally the munitions which they deploy (anti-missile systems) are then presented. And lastly the relatively recently introduced technology of Unmanned Aerial Systems is discussed, reviewing reconnaissance, attack and suicide UAV's.

MODERN FIGHTER AIRCRAFT

American Fighter Aircraft

The F-15 Eagle was the first true air superiority fighter. Since its introduction in 1976 into the United States Airforce (USAF) regular advancements have been integrated into the aircraft, producing the F-15 A/B and F-15 C/D models. The most modern configuration of the aircraft is the F-15E Strike Eagle, an all-weather multirole strike fighter. While the F-15 was originally designed as an air superiority fighter, the lack of peer-on-peer opponents resulted in the latest version of the aircraft being optimized for a ground attack role. Many air combat fighters in the US inventory have been successfully converted to the ground attack role, including the F-14 and F-16. The large engines of fighters are conducive to the carrying of heavy payloads. Produced since 1989, over 500 of the F-15E configuration have been built at a cost of $100 million USD each. The F-15E can be most readily discerned from other F-15 variants by the dark grey camouflage used to conceal its low altitude strike flight path, its tandem (dual) seating in the cockpit and the presence of extended range conformal fuel tanks.

An F-15E Strike Eagle
Credit: http://3.bp.blogspot.com/

The dual seating provides for a weapons systems officer (WSO) to relieve the pilot of excess workload. The WSO operates the air-to-ground avionics, including radar, electronic warfare, thermographic cameras, aircraft and weapons status, threats, target selection and mapping. The WSO can also assume controls and fly the aircraft in the case of the pilot becoming incapacitated. The F-15E is equipped with a APG-82 Active Electronically Scanned Array (AESA) radar. This unit enables the aircraft to perform ground suppression, precision ground strike, electronic warfare, anti-satellite missile launching and anti-ballistic missile-missile launching roles. While AESA radar can only scan for ground targets or air targets at one time, the WSO can save a ground scan and then hand back over control of the radar to the pilot to perform air sweeps. The

WSO can then proceed to engage the acquired and saved ground targets while the pilot engages any detected air targets.

The F-15E is also equipped with a AN/AAQ-13 navigation pod which contains a terrain-following radar and a forward-looking infrared system. The radar permits the pilot to fly very close to the ground and to even fly the plane in an autopilot terrain-following mode. The infrared system is known as Low-Altitude Navigation and Targeting Infrared for Night (LANTIRN). This system is used by the WSO to acquire, track and engage ground targets. It is particularly useful when operating at night or under adverse weather conditions. Facilitating with a laser designator, the infrared system can engage targets up to 10 mi (16 km) from the aircraft.

The F-15E is designed to independently perform high-speed interdiction missions without requiring escort aircraft to provide anti-aircraft or electronic warfare coverage. Defense of the F-15E against attack is provided by the aircraft maneuverability as well as by an electronic warfare system (TEWS). The system permits the WSO to operate and co-ordinate all electronic countermeasures that the aircraft possesses. These are extensive and include radar warning receivers, radar jammer, chaff and flare dispensers and the radar itself. The aircraft can also carry a ALQ-131 ECM pod on the centerline pylon to provide enhanced electronic warfare. F-15E's were deployed during Iraqi, Afghani, Syrian and Libyan conflicts and used to perform deep strike missions against high-value targets, as well as to provide close air support for ground troops and to conduct combat air patrols.

Other variants of the F-15 under consideration are the proposed F-15X and F-15EX, enhanced versions of the standard F-15C/D fighter configuration and the F-15E fighter-bomber configuration. Such variants of existing platforms are being considered because of their relatively low price-tag when compared to the comparatively expensive F-35. There remain many missions against opponents that do not possess sophisticated anti-aircraft capabilities and therefore for which stealth in not required. F-15's are less expensive to build and maintain than F-35's, as well as able to carry a greater payload. Another interesting option is to use F-15's to supplement attacking F-35's as a 'weapons truck'. In this approach the F-15 would trail behind advancing F-35's, which use their stealth to penetrate enemy defenses and identify targets. Co-ordinates for these targets would then be fed to the F-15's, which could then engage those targets with their large payload of long-range weapons.

The United States Navy's (USN) primary combat aircraft is the F/A-18 Hornet. Able to operate from the decks of aircraft carriers, the Hornet is a dual engine multirole all-weather combat aircraft (thus the designation F/A for Fighter/Attack). Maneuverability of the aircraft was enhanced in the design by introducing fly-by-wire flight controls and leading edge extensions, which permit a steeper angle of attack before stalling occurs. Roles for the aircraft include fleet air defense, fighter escort, air interdiction, close air support, suppression of enemy air defenses and aerial reconnaissance. Avionics of the F/A-18C/D (C is single seat while D is dual seat) were upgraded to include a jammer, synthetic aperture ground mapping radar, Hughes AN/AAR-5 thermal navigation pod and the Loral AN/AAS-38 NITE Hawk FLIR (forward looking infrared array) targeting pod.

The USN needs to continually modernize their capabilities and selected the F-35C to replace their aging F/A-18's. But as the F-35C was still under development the Navy chose to buy the F/A-18E Super Hornet as an interim solution. A 4.5 generation fighter/bomber introduced in 1999, the Super Hornet offers many capabilities beyond its predecessor. There are two configurations, the single-seat F/A-18E and the two-seat F/A-18F. The former is optimized for aerial combat while the two-seat version has a Weapon Systems Officer (WSO) to take on the heavy workload of synchronizing ground attack missions from the pilot who must focus on flying and possible aerial threats.

The Super Hornet is 25% larger than the original Hornet, has engines that are 35% more powerful and has increased fuel capacity, offering a 41% extended mission range. The leading edge extensions were enlarged to provide improved aerodynamic performance. The flight controls of the Super Hornet are a quadruplex digital fly-by-wire system which can correct flight characteristics to account for various levels of battle damage that might occur to the aircraft. Avionics were enhanced to include the APG-79 active electronically scanned array (AESA) radar and the joint helmet mounted cueing system, which permits high off-boresight missile cuing. This is facilitated with the AN/ASQ-

228 ATFLIR (Advanced Targeting Forward Looking Infrared) electro-optical sensor and laser designator.

The F/A-18F Super Hornet. Note the broad leading edge extensions.
Credit: https://without-the-love-fanfiction.blogspot.com/

The radar cross-section (RCS) of the F/A-18E is significantly reduced as compared to the F/A-18C/D, particularly from the front and rear perspectives. This was achieved by changing the design of the engine inlets so that they scatter rather than reflect radar waves, and by adding reflectors in the inlet tunnel to avoid radar from deflecting off the fan blades. RCS is also reduced through the use of serrations, perforated panels and smoother joints, transitions and corners, features shown to reduce radar reflection. Survivability of the aircraft in a hostile environment has also been improved through the addition of various defensive countermeasures. These include the AN/ALR-67(V)3 radar warning receiver, the AN/ALE-47 countermeasures dispenser (flares/chaff), the AN/ALE-50 towed decoy and the AN/ALQ-214 Integrated Defensive Countermeasures (IDECM) system. This last system has threat receivers that then employ jammers as required.

Russian Fighter Aircraft

The most modern and capable Russian fighter aircraft is the 4.5 generation Su-35 Flanker-E (NATO designation). A multi-purpose air superiority fighter, it is able to perform both air combat and precision ground strike missions. The Su-35 entered service with the Russian Airforce in 2009 at a unit cost of approximately $82 million USD. The single seat Su-35 was an evolutionary development from the earlier Su-27 Flanker, along with the tandem seat Su-34 ground attack platform and the Su-33, which is able to be operated from aircraft carriers. The Russian's prefer the give each of their aircraft a unique identification as they evolve, where in the West we more typically simply apply a model designation (i.e., F-15E, F/A-18C/D, F-35B).

The Su-35 provides significant enhancements over the earlier Su-27 Flanker, with improved avionics, engines and airframe. The cockpit and weapons-control systems were completely redesigned to accommodate the enhanced situational awareness and fire control integration. While leading-edge extensions were added to improve maneuverability by reducing buffeting at high angles of attack (AOA), increasing the AOA before stall occurs, and by strengthening the airframe so that the aircraft can sustain 10 G loading. The aircraft is capable of supercruise, has fly-by-wire-controls and a relaxed stability design. The Su-35 also has 3-D thrust vectoring, giving the aircraft what the Russian's refer to as super-maneuverability.

Su-35 Flanker-E
Credit: www.armytimes.com

These upgrades provide the relatively large and heavy air-superiority fighter excellent dog-fighting capabilities, with the ability to make abrupt sharp turns at high velocities. The Su-35 is one of the few aircraft in the world able to perform the so-called "Cobra" maneuver, whereby the aircraft can briefly be pitched up to 120 degrees such that it is flying with its nose past the vertical while maintaining forward momentum. This gives the pilot an opportunity to fire a missile at an opponent who would not otherwise be in their line-of-fire. The disadvantage of performing such a maneuver is obviously a loss of speed, which Western air combat philosophy prefers to preserve.

The weapons control system of the Su-35 is based around a multi-function N011 Bars phased-array radar with pulse-Doppler tracking. This allows the radar to detect targets below the horizon, providing the ability to engage ground targets. The N011 Bars is capable of simultaneously tracking fifteen targets and is able to direct missiles toward six targets at the same time. A further upgrade available for the Su-35 is the N035 Irbis-E passive electronically scanned array (PESA) radar. This radar is able to detect aircraft and other aerial targets to a range of 250 miles (400 km) and can track thirty targets simultaneously while engaging up to eight of these. This multi-function radar also provides high-resolution imagery of ground targets in the synthetic aperture mode.

The Su-35 also has an OLS-35 opto-electronic targeting system with infrared search and tracking (IRST). IRST permits aircraft to search for opponents using passive sensors only. This avoids having to activate the radar unit, the electronic signature of which can reveal the aircrafts presence and position. IRST however has only limited range as compared to conventional radar. Infrared signatures also do not inherently contain information regarding the range, direction and velocity of a detected target and are therefore supplemented with a laser rangefinder to assist in producing accurate firing solutions.

An electronic countermeasure (ECM) suite comes standard on the Su-35. Known as the L175M Khibiny-M, the system operates by interfering with an opponent's radar tracking functions as well as the radar guidance system of launched missiles. Digitally generated radio signals of the same frequencies as those used by the opponent's radar units are directed toward the opponent. These in turn disorient guidance systems by creating excessive background white noise. The Su-35 also has a rearward mounted N012 self-defense radar located in the tail boom. This provides the aircraft radar coverage with a rearward projection. While the radar cross-section (RCS) of the Su-35 has been reduced by employing radar absorbing materials along edges that produce high radar reflectivity. Decreased RCS reduces the range at which an opponent's radar can detect, track and engage the aircraft.

The Su-35 is available in export models and has so far been sold to China. This sale was considered controversial within Russia as China has previously reverse engineered Russian fighter aircraft that they bought. Namely, the Chinese stripped down Su-27SK and Su-33's and from this analysis created their own versions of the aircraft, which they named the J-11B and the J-15. To address the concern Russia acquired a promise from China's not to reverse engineer the Su-35. However this promise is presumably worth appreciably less than the paper it is written on. Russia was cash strapped when it agreed to the sale, but in general it is not good policy to sell military or civilian tech to China.

Another capable modern Russian fighter is the MiG-35 Fulcrum-F. Developed from the MiG-29M, the MiG-35 offers significantly enhanced avionics and weapon systems, as well as a greater range, enhanced payload and reduced radar cross-section. Introduced into service with the Russian military in 2019, the multirole 4.5 generation fighter was designed with a focus on close-quarters aerial combat while maintaining decent ground attack capabilities. Single and dual seat options are available. Smaller, lighter and less expensive than the Su-35, the MiG-35 is powered by two FADEC RD-33MK Morskaya Osa turbofans but lacks the 2D thrust vectoring nozzles. As with other Russian built aircraft the MiG-35 is available for international sale and orders have been placed by Egypt and Iraq.

The MiG-35 is equipped with the Phazotron Zhuk-AE active electronically scanned array (AESA) radar, the first Russian fighter aircraft to receive this enhanced radar unit. It can detect objects with a small RCS and can track up to 30 individual targets simultaneously. It is able to engage up to 6 of these as air targets or 4 as ground targets at the same time. The radar transmits over a wide range of frequencies, making it far more challenging to jam with Electronic Counter Measures (ECM). While a MSP-418KE compact active jammer pod can be added to one of the 10 available mounting hardpoints to provide the aircraft its own ECM jamming capabilities.

In addition to the radar unit the MiG can detect targets in the infrared using its OLS-UEM electro-optical targeting station. This system provides both forward-looking infrared (FLIR) for detection of air targets as well as a lookdown capability to detect ground and sea targets. The lookdown feature can also detect air targets flying close to the ground for concealment, such as tactical bombers and cruise missiles. Airborne targets can be detected to a range of 33 miles (55 km), sea targets to 24 miles (40 km) and ground targets out to 12 miles (20 km). The system is also equipped with a TV camera and multimode laser rangefinder with a 12 mile (20 km) range to assist in determining target distance, direction and velocity.

The dual seat version of the MiG-35. The co-pilot assists with ground attack operations.
Credit: www.gladiusds.com

It should be kept in mind that Russia tends to exaggerate their military systems capabilities as a marketing tool to promote international sales, and therefore their claims should always be taken with a grain of salt. Poor performance and reliability issues still tend to plague Russian built equipment. In 2007 a competition was held in India to compare the capabilities of modern fighters that India was interested in procuring. The aircraft involved included the pre-production MiG-35 along with the F-16 Fighting Falcon, F/A-18E/F Super Hornet, Eurofighter Typhoon, Dassault Rafale and Saab JAS 39 Gripen. The MiG-35 was removed from the competition due to deficiencies identified in both the aircraft's radar and engines. This suggests that Russia still lags behind their Western competitors in these key areas with regards to both engineering and manufacturing. The Russian invasion of Ukraine has also repeatedly demonstrated to the world the inadequacies of Russian military equipment and has presumably irrevocably undermined their credibility as a reputable source for international arms sales.

European Fighter Aircraft

The Eurofighter Typhoon is a 4.5 generation multirole fighter developed by a consortium of European partners. The UK, Germany, Italy and Spain each contributed to the design and the fabrication of the aircraft. The Typhoon was principally designed as an air superiority fighter, intended to be able to engage Russian aircraft as an agile dogfighter. The Eurofighter was also given the flexibility to operate as a multirole aircraft to fulfill all possible mission profiles that might be required into the foreseeable future. Introduced in

2003 at a cost of about $180 million USD each, the aircraft has also seen exports to Saudi Arabia, Oman, Kuwait and Qatar.

The aircraft is of a canard delta wing design and is powered by dual engines. The canard delta wing configuration gives the Eurofighter excellent supersonic flight characteristics. The design also provides high maneuverability at subsonic speeds by utilizing a relaxed stability design together with a quadruplex digital fly-by-wire control system. The Eurojet EJ200 engines provide 13500 lbf (60 kN) of thrust each, with this increasing by 50% when afterburners are applied. The engines provide for a supercruise capability and include many advanced technologies such as single crystal turbine blades, wide chord aerofoils, digital controls, health monitoring and a convergent/divergent exhaust nozzle.

The cockpit of the Typhoon is unique in that it lacks conventional instruments to provide the pilot flight information. Rather, there are three full color multi-function head-down displays (MHDD), a head-up display (HUD) and a Helmet Mounted Symbology System (HMSS) that alters displayed data depending upon the orientation of the pilot's head. The system integrates data from the radar, the forward looking infrared (FLIR) viewer, the MIDS and the aircraft warning system. Commands are issued via voice and hands-on throttle and stick controls (Voice+HOTAS), softkeys and cursor, Direct Voice Input (DVI) command and manual data-entry facility (MDEF) located on the glareshield.

The Typhoon has integrated additional safety override features to protect the pilot from crashing. At the press of an emergency button by the pilot in the event of pilot injury or disorientation the typhoon's Flight Control System will assume control of the aircraft and stabilize its flight, orienting the aircraft into a level flight path with a slight climb rate at 300 knots. As well there is an Automatic Low-Speed Recovery system (ALSR) which keeps the aircraft from stalling at low speeds or high angles of attack, automatically adjusting the flight control surfaces and engine speed as required.

The Eurofighter Typhoon.
Credit: https: http://www.mjaviation.co.uk/

The Typhoon uses an AESA radar that is integrated with a Multifunction Advanced Data Link (MADL). Through this system radar target and threat assessment data can be shared among aircraft. The radar unit of one aircraft can also detect reflected radio waves emitted from another Typhoon's radar. This allows one aircraft to illuminate the environment with its radar while other aircraft in the area are able to operate their own radar in a passive receiver mode only. This is significant as operating a radar unit provides the opponent awareness of not only the operators existence, but also their precise location and range. A remote Typhoon can therefore illuminate targets from the rear for forward aircraft which remain undetected. These can then launch missiles at the targets while themselves remaining inconspicuous.

Along with the radar unit the Eurofighter is also equipped with a sophisticated passive infrared search and tracking system. Able to discern subtle variations in temperature at long ranges, the infrared system can detect and track both air and land targets. Up to 200 targets can be tracked together and the output from the infrared sensors can be overlaid directly onto the pilot's helmet mounted sight. This allows for off-boresight missile launches toward targets that are not in line with the aircrafts flight path, such as those above or below the aircraft, or to its port or starboard side.

The aircraft are also equipped with a sophisticated defensive suite named Praetorian. The system monitors both air and surface threats and automatically reacts to these as detected, with the ability to respond to multiple threats simultaneously. Threats are detected via Radar Warning Receivers (RWR), Missile Warning System (MWS) and Laser Warning Receivers (LWR) distributed across the aircrafts surface. Sensor fusion of all data sources is provided through an Attack and Identification System (AIS), significantly reducing monitoring workload for the pilot while increasing their situational awareness. Countermeasures include chaff and flare dispensers, active decoys and ECM jammers. The jammers are composed of 16 AESA antenna array assemblies and 10 radomes. These have powerful focused radiators which generate extended band coverage. The AIS will also automatically reduce electronically generated emissions from the aircraft with the detection of a threat. The electromagnetic signature of an aircraft can be used by opponents and their missiles to better home in on the aircraft, so reducing this electromagnetic output reduces the aircrafts visibility.

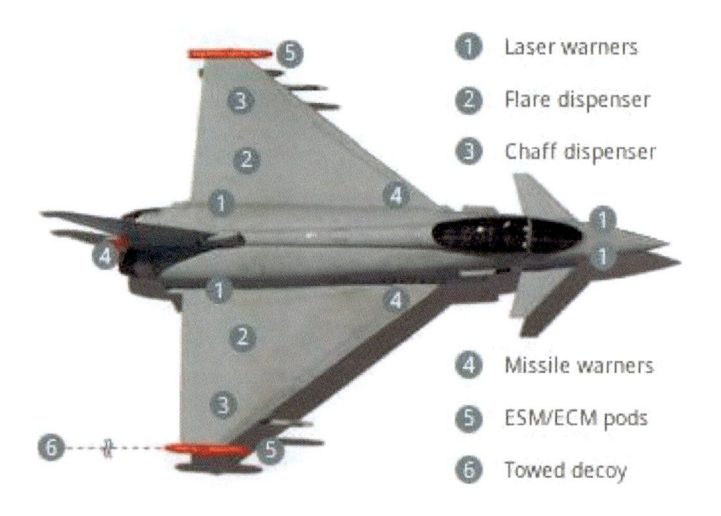

① Laser warners
② Flare dispenser
③ Chaff dispenser
④ Missile warners
⑤ ESM/ECM pods
⑥ Towed decoy

Defensive Aid Suite Distribution of the Eurofighter Typhoon.
Credit: https: www.eurofighter.com

Similar to other 4.5 generation aircraft, the Radar Cross-Section (RCS) of the Typhoon is appreciably lower than was typical for previous 4th generation aircraft. This was achieved by both geometric considerations and material selection. The jet inlet has a S-duct shape to conceal the highly reflective fan blades. Weapons are recessed into the fuselage to reduce their revealed reflective surfaces. Surfaces of the aircraft are highly contoured and swept to reduce radar reflectivity. And Radar-Absorbent Materials (RAM) were selectively applied on highly reflective surfaces such as wing leading edges, intake edges, rudder surrounds and strakes.

There are plans to make modifications to the Typhoon design to further enhance its performance. These include increasing engine thrust, adding Thrust Vectoring Control (TVC) nozzles to enhance maneuverability, adding Conformal Fuel Tanks (CFTs) to increase range and reshaping various features of the wings and fuselage to increase lift by 25%. These changes are intended to improve turn rate, turning radius, roll rate and maximum AOA. Known as "knife-fight in a phone box" turning capabilities, achieving this level of maneuverability would put the Eurofighter on par with other dog-fighter capable aircraft like the MiG-29, the F/A-18E/F and the F-16.

The Swedish JAS-39 Gripen is another European advanced multirole fighter designed to hold its own against Russian aircraft. First introduced in 1996, the Gripen is currently operating with the Swedish, South African, Brazilian, Czech Republic, Hungarian and Thai air forces. The cost of the aircraft is relatively inexpensive compared to many of its contemporaries at $30 to 60 million a unit, based on the level of sophisticated options selected. Similar to the

Typhoon, the Gripen is of a canard and delta wing configuration with relaxed stability design and fly-by-wire flight controls. The latest version of the single seat single engine aircraft is the E-series. It has an operational range of 810 miles (1300 km), a maximum takeoff weight of 35,300 lbs (16,000 kg), is capable of supercruise and a maximum Angle-of-Attack (AOA) of 80 degrees.

JAS-39 Gripen with the Brazilian air force.
Credit: https: www.parkflyersinternational.com

The Gripen is equipped with avionics integrated through a digital data bus to provide efficient sensor fusion through the Ternav tactical navigation system. The system is able to share data with both other aircraft and ground stations. Primary avionics consists of a Raven ES-05 active electronically scanned array (AESA) radar and the Skyward-G infrared search and track (IRST) sensor, enabling both air and ground attacks. Targets are tracked through a 'best sensor dominates' system, in which the computer automatically selects the best data available and presents this to the pilot. This significantly reduces pilot workload and provides enhanced situational awareness.

The Rafale is a French designed and built 4.5 generation multirole fighter. The dual engine aircraft was first introduced in 2001 at a unit cost of $250 million USD and is used by France, India, Greece, Qatar and Egypt. The aircraft is able to perform air superiority, interdiction, reconnaissance, ground support, in-depth ground attack, anti-ship launch platform and nuclear deterrence missions. The Rafale is available in three variants; the single seat Rafale C, the twin seat Rafale B and the single seat carrier based Rafale M. The French operate the aircraft from both air bases and their three aircraft carriers, with the twin seat configuration being preferred for ground strike and reconnaissance missions. The Rafale has already proven itself combat effective while in service over Afghanistan, Libya, Mali, Iraq and Syria.

The Rafale follows suit with other European modern fighter aircraft in utilizing a delta wing design facilitated with all-moving canards, fly-by-wire flight controls and relaxed stability. The aircraft is capable of supercruise and has excellent agility characteristics, with the structure able to withstand forces of up to +9g and -3.6g. Avionics include direct voice input, an RBE2 AA active electronically scanned array (AESA) radar and an infra-red search and track (IRST) sensor. Radar cross-section is reduced by including features that conceal the highly radar reflective surfaces such as the turbine blades. The aircraft has an integrated defensive-aids system known as SPECTRA, offering detection, jamming and the launching of decoys to provide protection against threats.

The French Rafale. Similarities to the Typhoon and Gripen are evident.
Credit: http:time.com

Indian Fighter Aircraft

Sophisticated modern fighter aircraft are also being developed by many other nations outside of the US, Russia and Europe. China, India, Japan, Taiwan and Iran each have their own fighter aircraft development programs. The Tejas is an Indian designed 4.5 generation multirole aircraft.

The single engine fighter was introduced in 2015 at a unit cost of between $24 and $42 million USD, depending upon options selected. The Tejas is currently in operation with both the Indian Air Force and Indian Navy. A relatively small and light aircraft compared to its contemporaries, the aircraft is designed as a tailless compound delta wing together with a single vertical stabilizer. The design includes relaxed static stability and fly-by-wire flight controls. These features provide excellent maneuverability to the aircraft. The flight control surfaces are powered by hydraulic actuators with dual redundancy in the hydraulics and quad redundancy in the electrical system.

The Tejas incorporates a multi-mode radar, multi-functional displays and a helmet-mount display and sight cueing system. The EL/M-2032 radar features look-up/look-down/shoot-down modes, low/medium/high pulse repetition frequencies, platform motion compensation, Doppler beam-sharpening, moving target indication, doppler filtering, rane-Doppler ambiguity resolution, scan conversion and online self-diagnostics. The electronic warfare suite offers a radar warning receiver, missile approach warning, laser warning receiver, infrared and ultraviolet missile warning sensors, self-protection jammer, chaff and flare dispenser, an electronic countermeasures suite and a towed radar decoy. The aircraft also possesses stealth features including composite material construction, a Y-duct engine inlet and the use of RAM's over high reflectivity surfaces.

In the design of the Tejas India placed an emphasis on expanding their domestic ability to produce modern military aircraft. Therefore very few of the aircraft's components are imported. The downside of this approach for a developing nation is that the resulting aircraft is not necessarily as capable as it potentially could have been. A 2015 review of the aircraft by the IAF concluded that the Tejas did not meet their requirements with regards to the radar warning receiver, missile approach warning and engine power. These are deficiencies that are hoped to be addressed in future versions of the aircraft.

Tejas light fighter.
Credit: https://learnbyexample.in

5th Generation Aircraft

While possessing a reduced Radar Cross-Section (RCS) compared to prior generation fighters, 4.5 generation aircraft still lack true stealth. As such, they would not be able to survive long in an intense modern battlespace with sophisticated radar and anti-aircraft missile technology.

This is evident in Ukraine, where modern 4.5 generation Russian fighters cannot achieve air dominance because the anti-aircraft missile systems Russia previously sold to the Ukrainians can shoot them down with relative ease. Therefore 5th generation aircraft must possess stealth, which is to say, a very very small RCS, as well as a significantly reduced infrared and electromagnetic signature. Before we review particular 5th generation aircraft, first let's discuss how stealth is achieved in aircraft.

There are a number of approaches that can be applied. To start, the shape of the aircraft can be configured such that it reflects a very small proportion of incoming radar waves back to the receiving antenna. This concept was conceived of soon after the advent of radar. But the calculations required to analyze reflectivity over the entire surface of the aircraft from all angles is exhaustive. Therefore it was not until the development of modern ultra-fast computers that performing the calculations required was reasonable. It is for this reason that the first stealth aircraft, the F-117, consisted of simple flat facetted faces – this was all the computers of the time were capable of analyzing. It is also the reason that modern Russian and Chinese stealth aircraft only offer reasonable stealth from a direct front on perspective – they are still lacking in their computational capabilities as compared to the United States and Western Europe.

Radar reflectivity can also be reduced by applying to the aircraft a coating of radar absorbing materials. Such materials are often applied to highly reflective surfaces which cannot be mitigated through contouring. The use of composite materials also reduces the overall reflectivity of the aircraft. As well radar reflectivity can be reduced simply by removing aspects of an aircraft design that tend to generate strong radar reflections, such as highly angled components. These include weapon mounting pylons, external sensors and turbine blades. Through surface contouring, applying radar absorbing coatings, embedding sensors below the aircraft surface, using internal weapons bays and by altering the geometry of air inlet nozzles, 5th generation aircraft are able to significantly reduce their RCS.

Stealth also requires reducing the infrared and electromagnetic signature of the aircraft. Infrared radiation is produced by any heat generated by the aircraft. While electromagnetic radiation sources include radio transmissions, radar and even system avionics. Both infrared and electromagnetic emissions can be detected by an opponent's sensors and therefore used to track the aircraft. Infrared signature is reduced by altering the design of exhaust outlet nozzles, placing the engines closer to the upper surface of the aircraft. While electromagnetic emissions are reduced by using pulsed communications, directional radar or by simply not turning on the radar unit. For a sensor designed to detect radio waves, the powerful radio waves created by a radar unit are similar to the light shining from a lighthouse – they act as a beacon in the sky indicating the presence of the emitting aircraft.

Other characteristics common in 5th generation aircraft are encrypted and cyber protected avionics, sensor fusion, networked communications and electronic warfare systems. Cyber protection and electronic jammers offer the aircraft levels of protection beyond that provided by stealth alone, where networking permits platforms to co-ordinate activities much more closely. Aircraft are able share sensor information with other aircraft, as well as ground and ship-based systems, increasing situational awareness all across the battlespace. Networking additionally lets aircraft hand off tasks to other aircraft or systems, providing for an entire battlegroup to behave essentially as a single war machine.

Stealth aircraft design, together with the development of precision weaponry, proved its worth during the opening stages of the Persian Gulf War. The Iraqi city of Baghdad was protected by a sophisticated air defense system estimated to be four-fold more extensive than that which so effectively protected the city of Saigon from American airpower during the Vietnam War. Yet precision weapons launched from American stealth F-117's eliminated the cities command and control centers along with the air defense systems within days without incurring a single loss in the process. This is turn opened the Iraqi's up to follow-up attacks by traditional fighter-bomber aircraft and ultimately to the ground invasion.

American Stealth Fighters

The F-22 Raptor was the first stealth air superiority fighter, following in the steps of the novel if ungainly stealth F-117 Nighthawk ground attack aircraft. Introduced in 2005, the multirole F-22 is able to perform air dominance, dog-fighting and ground attack missions. There are currently almost 200 Raptor's in active service with the US Air Force. These have seen service patrolling Iranian airspace, dropping munitions in Syria and performing surveillance and close air support missions in the Middle East. It was the first aircraft created that offered stealth, supercruise, supermaneuvrability, thrust vectoring and sensor fusion all together in one platform. Revolutionary in aircraft design rather than just evolutionary, the F-22 both introduced and defined the notion of a 5th generation fighter.

The F-22 remains by far the most capable fighter aircraft ever built. The single-seat twin engine all weather fighter can achieve Mach 1.8 in supercruise, is virtually invisible to radar and is able to engage in combat at over Mach 1.5 at altitudes of greater than 50,000 feet (15,000 meters). There has never been another aircraft created with near comparable capabilities. This is because the aircraft is in essence an evaluation platform for all of these new technologies. But such an endeavor of course comes at a very cost per aircraft. Therefore new platforms, such as the F-35 Lightening II, are essentially toned-down versions of the F-22. They preserve the characteristics considered essential in a 5th generation multi-role fighter and remove the features that are not essential but drive the cost up exponentially.

The F-22's maneuverability is among the best in the world for fighter aircraft. This was achieved through a combination of thrust vectoring engines, relaxed stability design, wing-shape design and the integration of multiple independently adjustable control surfaces. The aircraft's weapons are loaded into an internal weapon bay to reduce parasitic drag, as well as RCS. These characteristics give the F-22 the ability to fly with angles of attack of 60 degrees and to perform aerial combat maneuvers such as the Herbst maneuver (J-turn) and Pugachev's Cobra. But unlike many other high maneuverability aircraft, pilots were quick to comment that the aircraft remains easy to control, a breeze to fly and inherently resistant to unstable flight. Constructed of advanced materials such as titanium and carbon fiber composite, the frame of the F-22 is designed to withstand the intense accelerations and heat inputs associated with performing extreme combat maneuvers.

F-22 Raptor
Credit: https://theaviationgeekclub.com/

In addition to high performance maneuverability, the F-22 also integrates extensive sensor fusion technology. The avionics equipment on all prior aircraft operated as individual systems and often required monitoring by a dedicated weapons system operator. With sensor fusion all data collected by the aircrafts sensors is analyzed by a powerful computer. Relevant information is sorted and presented to the pilot. This provides the pilot full situational awareness, permitting them to respond quickly to threats and to opportunities as they present themselves. Systems integrated into the sensor fusion suite aboard the Raptor include the AN/ALR-94 electronic warfare system, the AN/AAR-56 infrared and ultraviolet Missile Launch Detector (MLD), the AN/APG-77 active electronically scanned array (AESA) radar and the Communication / Navigation / Identification (CNI) system.

Each of these avionics systems is an impressive feat of technology in itself. The MLD deploys six sensors around the periphery of the aircraft to provide full spherical detection of an air or ground launched missile and to determine if the threat is directed at the F-22. While the ALR-94 consists of a passive radar detector and 30 receiving antennae to provide advance notice of any radar activity directed toward the aircraft. With a detection range of over 250 nautical miles, the system can discern between different types of radar and determine the orientation of the radar source to within 2° in both azimuth and elevation. Stealth aircraft are not invisible to radar, but are merely more challenging to detect using radar. Radar can only detect a stealth aircraft at close range and even then have difficulty acquiring the location of the aircraft with sufficient precision to guide anti-aircraft missiles toward it. The ALR-94 therefore determines if the detected radar presents any threat to the F-22 (i.e., does it have any chance of detecting, acquiring and tracking the aircraft) and if so provides the pilot with a recommended response, such as executing defensive maneuvers or to launch a missile at the enemy radar.

The radar of the F-22, the AN/APG-77 AESA, has a range of 150 miles (241 km). Active electronically scanned array radar (AESA) are able to operate in multiple modes at the same time, have no moving parts and are capable of projecting a tight radar beam with rapid scanning. The radar unit of the F-22 utilizes a low probability of intercept (LPI) capacity. LPI spreads the energy of each radar pulse out over several frequencies so as not to trip the radar warning receivers that other aircraft carry. The AN/APG-77 can also confine its search to a narrow beam, reducing the probability of detection by an opponent as well as increasing the range to 250 miles (400 km). It is able to track multiple targets simultaneously, under day/night and adverse weather conditions. The radar is resistant to jamming as it fluctuates in operating frequency at a rate of over 1000 times per second, making it challenging for an opponent to generate and direct at the F-22 an overwhelming 'white noise' signal over the full spectrum range used.

While resistant to being jammed, the AN/APG-77 can be actively used as a radar jammer. The unit is used to direct an Electronic Counter Measure (ECM) attack against an opponent by aiming a focused high energy beam of radio signals at the opposing aircraft to overload their radar receiver with an obscuring white noise signal. An upgrade to the radar of the F-22 was also introduced to improve its ground attack capabilities. Synthetic Aperture Radar (SAR) uses electromagnetic signals or "pings" to deliver a detailed 3D rendering of the terrain below, allowing for better target identification. Radar data can also be shared by the F-22 with other aircraft, permitting it to function as a mini-Airborne Warning and Control System (AWACS). This accommodates the handing off or coordination of attacks between aircraft.

Ultra-low radar reflectivity for the F-22 is provided along all aircraft surfaces for all radar transmission incident angles, with an emphasis being placed upon full optimization of stealth along the frontal arc of the aircraft. The aircraft was also designed to produce low radio frequency emissions, a low infrared signature, a low acoustic signature and reduced optical visibility. The F-22's flat thrust-vectoring nozzles help reduce the exhausts infrared emissions. Weapons are stored in internalized bays to reduce radar reflectivity from high-angled munition surfaces. To launch a weapon the bay doors open and close in less than a second, minimizing the duration for which the aircraft has an increased RCS.

The F-22 can carry up to 8 anti-aircraft missiles within the internalized bays to engage other aircraft. The Raptor is also armed with a M61A2 Vulcan 20 mm rotary cannon which has a retractable door to provide stealth. Ground attack munitions can also be carried within the internalized bays. The high cruising speed and operational altitude of the F-22 significantly enhances the range of these guided munitions compared to when deployed by other aircraft.

During testing an F-22 demonstrated its ability to drop a guided bomb at 50,000 feet (15,000 meters) while traveling at Mach 1.5 to successfully hit a moving target 24 miles (39 km) away. This represented an improvement in effective range for this munition of 50%. For missions not requiring stealth, hardpoints on the wings add capacity for an additional 20,000 lbs (9100 kg) of munitions and fuel. Full stealth is restored once the munitions and auxiliary fuel tanks have been released.

The stealth features of the F-22 are second to none, and this gives the edge to the F-22 in any aerial engagement. However, like other stealth aircraft the F-22 is optimized to reduce RCS from the front on perspective against high frequency radar, minimizing its detectability by opposing aircraft. Ground based radar, observing the F-22 from a non-front-on perspective and able to employ a broad range of radar frequencies including those in the low bands, may be able to sporadically detect stealth aircraft when they are close to the radar site. For this reason the F-22, as with other stealth aircraft, must fly routes that avoid travelling in close proximity to known radar installations. Stealth reduces observability to ground stations, but more critically avoids detection by other aircraft and makes it very challenging for both opposing aircraft and ground stations to achieve a lock-on to the stealth aircraft with their weapon systems.

The F-35 Lightening II Joint Strike Fighter is the successor of the F-22 and the first, as well as to date the only, mass produced 5th generation stealth aircraft. The less costly and more versatile F-35 was decided upon by the US Military over the more capable but higher cost F-22 to serve as the future common platform for the USAF, USN and United States Marine Corps (USMC). The F-35 is a single-seat, single-engine all-weather stealth multirole combat aircraft. Optimized for both the air superiority and ground strike roles, it is also highly effective at performing electronic warfare and reconnaissance missions. Over 600 of the aircraft have been constructed to date with more being produced off the assembly lines daily. The US plans to use the F-35 as their primary tactical aircraft, intending to procure more than 2400 of the aircraft over the coming years.

The Lightening II is available in three configurations; the Airforce's F-35A, the Marines short take-off and landing F-35B and the Navy's carrier operated F-35C. The multirole fighter entered service with the USMC in 2015, in 2016 with the USAF and with the USN in 2019. Designed under the Joint Strike Fighter (JSF) program, funding was provided by the United States along with their partners and allies in the UK, Italy, Australia, Canada, Norway, Denmark, the Netherlands and Turkey. Cost per aircraft ranges from $78 million USD for the basic Airforce unit up to $101 million for the more robust Marine Corps version. The aircraft is available for international sale to eligible allies at a cost of $133 million USD a unit. Israel, Poland and Singapore have each purchased the F-35 in addition to the JSF program partners.

A pair of F-35 Lightening II fighter jets in flight.
www.superiorwallpapers.com

A major task intended for the F-35 to perform is the suppression of enemy air defense capabilities. Similar to how the F-117 was employed during the Iraq war, this involves penetrating an opponent's radar screen and destroying their radar control and command infrastructure. This then clears the way for other aircraft to engage targets within the neutralized zone. To achieve this mission, as well as to fulfill its other intended roles, the F-35 was designed to possess low observability (stealth), advanced sensor fused avionics and long-range lethality. Stealth is achieved through airframe contouring, use of radar absorbing materials (RAM), internalized weapons bays and concealment of radio wave reflecting surfaces such as turbine blades. The RCS is significantly reduced over the 360 degree sphere of the aircraft against all radio frequencies, with a focus toward the front of the aircraft against high frequency radio emissions. It is said that the

RCS of the F-35 is similar to that generated by a golf ball, which is only slightly greater than that of the F-22, which is said to have a RCS equivalent to that of a marble. Like the F-22, the F-35 also has low detectability in the infrared, visual and radio frequency emission bands.

Much of the F-35's capabilities come from its comprehensive array of sophisticated avionics and sensor fusion. This provides the aircraft with network-centric warfare capabilities, including offering the pilot unprecedented situational awareness of the local battlespace as well as the ability to share that awareness with other aircraft. Each system has been integrated into the airframe such that upgrades can be incorporated as new technologies emerge. Key mission system sensors include AN/APG-81 active electronically scanned array (AESA) radar, AN/ASQ-239 Barracuda electronic warfare system, AN/AAQ-37 Distributed Aperture System (DAS), AN/ASQ-242 Communications, Navigation, and Identification (CNI) suite and AN/AAQ-40 Electro-Optical Targeting System (EOTS). The EOTS is mounted under the nose of the aircraft and provides laser targeting, forward looking infrared (FLIR) and long range infrared search and track (IRST).

The APG-81 radar can track multiple targets in the sky out to 150 miles (240 km) distance using rapid electronic scanning. While synthetic aperture radar provides for 3D ground mapping to identify and engage ground targets. Passive mode detection (radar is not transmitting but only receiving) can be selected so that the F-35 does not reveal its own position by directly generating radio emissions. In passive mode the radar still detects and tracks opponents either through radio waves generated by the target, or from radio reflections bouncing off of the target that originated from another friendly source. To further improve stealth the radar antenna on the F-35 is placed in a backward orientation, thus avoiding radar waves from being reflected off of its flat emitting/receiving surface.

The AAQ-37 DAS provides missile launch warning and tracking through six infrared sensors placed around the aircraft. And the ASQ-239 Barracuda provides early warning of any tracking radar which is directed toward the aircraft through placement of ten radio frequency antennas around the aircraft perimeter. Outputs from the radio frequency and infrared spectrum sensors are fused together to provide the pilot immediate awareness of any hostile actions being taken against the aircraft. In response to identified threats the Barracuda can actively jam the hostile radar source by permeating the unit with high intensity signals. This has the effect of blinding the receiving sensor by overloading them with broad spectrum white noise.

The pilot interfaces with the aircraft through a combination of visual cues, voice commands and touch screens. There is a 20" x 8" (50 cm x 20 cm) panoramic touchscreen which provides the pilot readouts of aircraft configuration and sensor readings. While the helmet visor displays critical flight, enemy contact and weapons lock-on information. Not only can the pilot see infrared and night vision projections over their field of view, but interfaces with externally mounted cameras permits the pilot to see through the aircraft structure virtually, providing them 360 hemispherical situational awareness of the battlespace. The system allows the pilot to fire missiles at any target observed on the visor even when the pilot is not looking forward. This high-angle off-boresight cuing is achieved by having information regarding the target location being fed directly to the missile seeker. Once launched the missile automatically changes direction to orient itself with the identified target. Such an amazing helmet of course does not come cheaply – each costs $400,000.

Similar to the F-22, weapons are stored within internalized weapons bays. This avoids the high angle surfaces of the munitions from behaving as strong radar reflectors, as occurs when they are mounted external to an aircraft. Whereas the F-22 can carry 8 anti-aircraft missiles, the F-35 can carry only 4. There is an effort underway to create a weapons rack that would increase this to 6. External hardpoints are also available for low stealth segments of missions, permitting an additional 12,500 lbs (5700 kg) of ordnance to be carried. This can include a combination of air-to-air and guided air-to-ground munitions. The F-35A is also armed with a 25 mm rotary cannon while the F-35B/C have no internally mounted gun but can opt to carry an externally mounted gun pod.

The F-35 is powered by a single Pratt & Whitney F135 turbofan that can generate 43,000 pound-force (191 kN) of thrust. While more fuel efficient than the engines of the F-22, the F135 does not provide true supercruise. Rather, the aircraft uses its afterburner to achieve supersonic flight and then is able to maintain its velocity without the afterburner.

The engine nozzle of the F-35B is able to swivel download to provide vertical thrust vectoring to achieve a short take off and vertical landing (STOVL) capability. Working together with a forward lift fan installed along the centerline, vectored engines provide the F-35B the helicopter like ability to descend vertically.

The F-35 was designed with relaxed stability and fly-by-wire controls to provide it with maneuverability comparable to that of the F-16 and F-18. As the primary missions envisioned for the F-35 do not involve close-in aerial combat, the very costly features of the F-22 that provide it with its extraordinary aerodynamic maneuverability were avoided. The philosophy employed with the design of the F-35 was to let the aircraft's stealth permit bringing the fight to the enemy without the enemy ever being aware of the aircraft's presence. This was aptly demonstrated by the Israeli's when they flew three of their F-35's (known as F-35I's) from Israel to the capital of Iran and back without their presence ever being detected by the Iranians.

Chinese Stealth Fighters

Russia and China have been playing catch-up since the advent of American stealth aircraft, recognizing that they will require aircraft with similar capabilities to compete in peer-on-peer actions. Russian efforts appear to be largely independent of US acquired technology and the American design approach. Chinese efforts on the other hand are largely based around stolen US technology and represent copies of American designs. To date both Chinese and Russian stealth aircraft remain poor examples of such aircraft and exist in only limited numbers. These aircraft can be thought of as developmental proto-types, as each nation familiarizes themselves with the technologies involved. Needless to say, Russian and Chinese efforts to develop stealth aircraft equivalent to their American counterparts can be expected to continue and to accelerate.

The J-20 Mighty Dragon is a Chinese 5th generation single-seat dual engine all-weather stealth air superiority fighter capable of ground strikes. Introduced in 2017, 50 aircraft had been built by the end of 2019 at an estimated unit cost of $100 million USD each. The aircraft is both quite large and unique in its appearance for a fighter aircraft. At first Western observers thought the J-20 to be a tactical bomber, appearing to be too large for an air superiority fighter. Large proportions for an aircraft are typically considered counter-productive to both achieving stealth and maneuverability. It is now thought that the aircraft is intended to act as a stand-off weapons platform, launching missiles at other aircraft over long ranges while remaining difficult to detect. Suitable targets would be an opponent's bombers, AWACS, fueling tankers and surveillance aircraft, where more agile aircraft can take effective evasive action when attacked over long distances.

J-20 Mighty Dragon
wall.alphacoders.com

The Chinese have not publicly disclosed details of the aircrafts avionics. The radar system is thought to be the indigenous KLJ-5 AESA. The J-20 also has an electro-optical/infrared targeting system consisting of six sensors placed around the aircraft to provide 360 degree hemispherical awareness. Similar to the F-35, sensor fusion combines infrared and radar data into a common format for the pilot to access. Data is displayed to the pilot on a 24 inch x 9 inch (61 cm x 23 cm) LCD touchscreen and a holographic heads-up display (HUD) unit. The J-20 also has a data-linked communication suite that can share data with other aircraft. The targeting sights are located on the helmet visor, allowing pilots to launch high off-boresight missile attacks. The aircraft can be thought of as a good first attempt to integrate 5th generation technologies into a single platform.

The J-20 stores its weapons within internal weapons bays operated with rapidly opening and closing bay doors. Up to six anti-aircraft missiles can be carried, or alternatively a small allotment of ground attack munitions can be accommodated. The anti-aircraft missiles used are large long-range types. The aircraft is not equipped with an internal autocannon and there are hardpoints on the wings to accommodate extended range fuel tanks, which are dropped prior to approaching a target to achieve maximum stealth. This configuration reinforces the conclusion that the primary role of the J-20 is as a low observable long-range stand-off anti-aircraft weapons platform and that it lacks the maneuverability required to effectively engage in close-quarter aerial combat.

Currently the J-20 is powered using Russian built jet engines. The J-20 was intended to be powered by an indigenously developed engine, but the Chinese continue to experience engineering and manufacturing issues related to producing compact powerful jet engines. As a result Russian built Saturn AL-31 engines are installed in the aircraft. The Chinese WS-15 powerplant currently remains under development, with design and quality issues continuing to plague fabrication efforts. Fully functional WS-15 engines are required if the J-20 is to be supercruise capable. Once the WS-15's are fielded, the aircraft will have a maximum speed of Mach 2.55, a combat range of 1200 miles (2000 km) and a maximum ceiling of 66,000 ft (20,000 meters).

The Chinese claim that the stealth provided by the J-20 is second to none, but this was received dubiously by Western analysts. The shape of the J-20 tends to suggest the front of the aircraft is a copy of the F-22 and therefore would have effective stealth characteristics from the front on perspective. The shape of the side and rear profiles of the aircraft however suggests significantly lower stealth performance. The front canards on the aircraft are inappropriate for a low-observable design, their high angles being significant radar wave reflectors. Generally it is felt that the aircraft only has a high level of stealth from the forward perspective, the view that would be presented to any aircraft that the J-20 was attacking. This is further evidence that its role is essentially a defensive one, intended to counter-attack approaching aircraft. The J-20 would become visible to an opponent's radar and present an easy target if viewed from any orientation other than front on, especially considering its limited ability to take abrupt defensive maneuvers.

The Chinese have also developed the much smaller FC-31 Gyrfalcon stealth fighter, also known as the J-35. In many regards it appears to be a copy of the F-35, with the exception that it is configured with dual engines. Developed through a private venture effort, to date only a few have been built for evaluation. Once fully matured, the company that developed the Gyrfalcon hopes to sell the JC-31 to China for use on their new aircraft carriers as well as to sell it on the international market. This is a very interesting development within China, where companies are developing their own military equipment independent of Chinese government oversight, while also wishing to offer their products for export sales. Marketed as a low-cost basic 5th generation fighter, the Gyrfalcon could become an affordable stealth option to developing nations.

The FC-31 has a twin-tailed configuration and many low-observable technologies incorporated within its design, including surface contouring and the use of Radar Absorbing Materials (RAM). The aircraft can carry PL-10 short range anti-aircraft missiles and PL-12 and PL-21 medium range anti-aircraft missiles within its internal weapons bays, but the quantity is unknown. With a maximum take-off weight of 55,000 lbs (25,000 kg) the aircraft has a combat radius of 746 miles (1,200 kg). This is a relatively short range, suggesting limited on-board fuel. US military sources believe that the J-31 is a well-designed aircraft and that it would be more than a match for existing Western 4th generation fighters. It is felt however that it remains a weak performer in terms of stealth, avionics and maneuverability as compared to the F-35.

Chinese FC-31 Gyrfalcon (J-35) stealth fighter – clearly a F-35 knock-off
Credit: thedrive.com

Russian Stealth Aircraft

The Su-57 Felon is a Russian single-seat twin-engine multirole stealth fighter, able to engage in both air combat and ground attack roles. The fighter offers supercruise, supermaneuverability, low observability features, advanced avionics and a defensive suite. With a combination of thrust vectoring and adjustable control surfaces the aircraft has excellent maneuverability, a cherished feature in aircraft produced by the Russians. It is able to achieve Mach 2, to fly at a high angle-of-attack (AOA) and to perform abrupt changes to its flight direction, with a robust airframe able to withstand 15 g loads. Powered by an upgraded version of the engines found on the Su-35, the thrust vectoring nozzles of the Su-57 are configured similarly to those of the Flanker-E, permitting thrust vectoring moments to be produced about all three rotational axes. The aircrafts supersonic range is 930 miles (1500 km), more than twice that of the Su-27.

It is thought that the Felon was designed as an air superiority counter-stealth fighter, able to get in close to opposing stealth aircraft and then defeat them through their high maneuverability in a dog-fight. To support this function the Su-57 mounts an internal 30 mm canon and stores up to six anti-aircraft missiles within internal weapons bays. Its high speed and operational altitude would also permit the aircraft to serve the role of a long-range strike platform against air, ground and naval targets. The concealed weapons bays can alternatively hold a range of air-to-surface precision strike missiles and bombs.

Su-57 Felon
Credit: www.key.aero

Sensors on the Su-57 include an electro-optical system, a X-band AESA radar and a multifunctional integrated radio electronic system (MIRES). This later system consists of a Beyelka radar and a Himalayas electronic countermeasure system. The system provides an infrared countermeasure against incoming heat seeking type missile threats, involving the automatic focusing of a modulated laser beam toward the missile to confuse or disrupt the missiles guidance sensor. The electro-optical system has a search and track turret mounted sensor that detects, identifies and tracks multiple targets through their visual, UV and IR signatures. The AESA radar has a side-looking feature, which can confuse an opponent with regards to the orientation of the Felon, as well as offering the Su-57 excellent high-off boresight missile launch capabilities. The pilot receives digital information from the various aircraft sensors through multiple 15 inch (38 cm) multi-functional LCD displays and a HUD unit, similar to the Su-35 configuration.

While all of this sounds fabulous on paper, the reality of the situation with regards to the Felon is a bit different. Development of the Su-57 has lagged appreciably behind that of the F-35 and even the J-20, both in terms of progress as well as in stealth offered. Stealth from the frontal perspective of the Felon is adequate, but generally lacking otherwise. As well development has been stalled by the lack of key combat systems. While Russia plans to produce a total of 28 of the fighters, with delivery having started in 2019, the aircraft appears to be more of a proto-typing exercise. Similar to the role that the F-22 served in the ultimate development of the F-35, the Su-57 incorporates all feasible technologies. It is presumed that the performance of the platform is to be evaluated and based upon lessons learned from testing of the Su-57, a more cost-effective Russian 5th generation fighter would be proposed for future development.

Similar to the Chinese, the Russians have also developed a smaller less expensive stealth fighter intended for the international export market, with the focus on selling second and third world nations stealth capable fighters that they can afford. The Russians call their latest development the Su-75 Checkmate. The single engine stealth aircraft is a light-weight fighter that has a reasonable combat load of seven tons, can attain speeds of Mach 1.8 and has a combat radius of 1860 miles (3000 km). Russia expects to be able to start delivering the fighter to customers by 2026, with potentially interested buyers including nations like Argentina, India, Vietnam and various African nations.

Not much has been revealed about the Checkmate to date but some general observations can be made. The Checkmate design includes an internal weapons bay, V-shape tail and divertless air intakes to reduce its RCS. The large wings of the aircraft imply that the Su-75 is meant to operate in high altitude air combat. The internal bays can accommodate five anti-aircraft missiles as well as air-to-surface munitions. The cockpit appears to be very similar to that of the Felon, with two 15 inch (38 cm) displays and a HUD. Avionics include an active phased array radar. In time we will learn more about the Checkmate, its capabilities, and its impact on the stealth aircraft market.

A prototype of Russia's new Sukhoi "Checkmate" fighter on display at the MAKS 2021 International Aviation and Space Salon, near Moscow.
Credit: www.riadanda.com

MODERN STRATEGIC BOMBERS

Stealth has not only become essential to the survival of fighter aircraft in the modern battlespace, but it is also a requirement for long-range bombers if they are to be able to complete their missions. Bombers are used to perform a range of missions including saturation bombing of target areas, executing precision strikes on high value targets and to deliver nuclear munitions against strategic assets. Critically, bombers offer a significantly less expensive means of striking enemy targets than employment of surface launched long-range ballistic missiles. The bomber essentially serves as transportation for the munition to the target, providing a less expensive means of delivery per munition than that associated with a long-range rocket system. With modern guidance systems and target-homing technologies even simple dumb bombs are now highly accurate and a single bomber can carry enough bombs to devastate a huge area or destroy large numbers of individual targets.

The relatively recent development of sophisticated radar and accurate long-range anti-aircraft missiles has rendered traditional bombers obsolete when facing even a near-peer opponent. The trend in this direction first became evident as long ago as the early 1970's with the loss of many B-52 bombers over North Vietnam from Soviet SA-2 missiles. Thereafter new designs sought to put the bombers at sufficiently great altitudes that they were beyond the reach of anti-aircraft missiles. But missile development kept pace and this approach became untenable, with the bombers remaining susceptible. The next approach was to fly bombers at very low altitudes, basically skimming over the tree tops at very high speeds. The notion was to remain below the detection limits of ground-based radar, to confuse airborne radar with the background clutter of terrain and to provide anti-aircraft missiles and fighter aircraft too little time to respond effectively to the incoming high-speed threat. A fine example of this approach is the British Vulcan.

The Avro Vulcan, a tree skimming bomber
Credit: www.loveplanes.co.uk

This approach proved successful for a while but the development of more sensitive ground based Doppler long range radar, together with millimeter wavelength airborne radar, provided a means for both early detection of incoming bombers and for fighter jets to track and target bombers against the background landscape. Simultaneous development of ultra-fast interceptors such as the MiG-25 and MiG-31, along with large fast air-launched anti-aircraft pursuit missiles, ensured that the fighters would also be able to catch up to penetrating bombers. Thereafter alternative solutions had to be contrived to preserve the bombers during an attack run. Supersonic low RCS bombers were paired with the launching of long-range munitions such as cruise missiles, glide bombs and air-launched ballistic missiles. This gave the bomber the advantage of being able to quickly penetrate enemy airspace, remain distant from air defenses while launching their long-range payload and to then rapidly return to friendlier skies.

The first of these 'low-observable' aircraft was the American B1 Lancer. While its stealth features were not as advanced as modern bombers, the B1 possessed only a small fraction of the RCS of previous bombers. The Lancer was designed to approach its target at supersonic speed at a low altitude and to launch long-range stand-off munitions such as cruise missiles. Its low RCS would keep it invisible to an opponent's radar at the range at which it launched its weapons. And by the time the opponents interceptors arrived at the launch location, the B1 was already long gone and far away. The Soviets in turn developed their equivalent version of the B1, the Tu-160 Blackjack. As impressive as they were, these aircraft proved to be still unacceptably vulnerable to ever advancing air defense systems. They also could not take advantage of the recently developed low cost high altitude deployable precision munitions, relying rather on the use of much more expensive long range weapons.

American B1 Lancer (top images) and Russian Tu-160 Blackjack (bottom images). The similarities in design are obvious.
Credit: www.defencetalk.com

The need therefore was for the development of a truly stealth bomber, one not with a low RCS but one essentially invisible to radar. The result was the American B-2 Spirit, by far the most recognized modern bomber. At a unit cost of over $2 billion USD a piece the B-2 became operational in 1997. The Spirit is capable of striking any target in the world from any point in the world. Most B-2 bombers operate out of Missouri and fly directly from there to their targets across the planet. To achieve its extremely high levels of stealth the aircraft takes advantage of radar dispersing geometry, composite materials and radar-absorbent materials. The aircraft was also one of the first to include new high-tech electronic avionics such as Terrain Following Radar, GPS navigation and streamlined satellite communication. It can deploy GPS-guided JDAM munitions, giving the bomber the never before seen role of a high altitude precision strike bomber. The B-2 is able to accurately drop JDAM bombs onto targets from altitudes so great that the opponent isn't even aware of there being a bomber in the sky above them.

The B-2 however is atrociously expensive to operate. With an operational cost of $163,000 USD an hour of flight time and the need for 60 man-hours of maintenance for each of those hours flown, the Spirit is therefore reserved for high priority missions. For this reason the US has developed a new stealth bomber which is essentially a technologically enhanced but lower cost version of the B-2, known as the B-21 Raider. The Raider also takes advantage of newly developed stealth technologies. While the B-2 was invisible to radar of its day, radar technologies have continued to evolve in the constant game of military research cat and mouse. This has resulted in the B-2 now being only nominally stealthy. The B-21 therefore incorporates additional stealth and avionics technologies developed through creation of the F-22 and F-35. This includes more effective but lower cost RAM, as well as sensor fusion with allied forces. This feature allows the B-21 to serve as a surveillance platform to ground forces and low flying fighter aircraft as it cruises above the battlefield awaiting co-ordinates for targets to engage.

The American B-2 Spirit Stealth Bomber.
Credit: www.dailymail.co.uk

The B-21 is projected to enter service in the mid 2020's. As compared to the price tag of $2 billion USD for a B-2, the B-21's are projected to cost only $670 million USD each, though we will have to wait and see if this target can be reached. Actual military costs often appreciably over-run optimist projections meant to satisfy bean counters and encourage development and procurement. The Airforce has requested the procurement of at least 100 Raiders to support their plan to retire many of their B-52 and B-1 bombers. The Defense Department often provides the various armed services fewer assets than requested though due to monetary constraints and the need to support other systems.

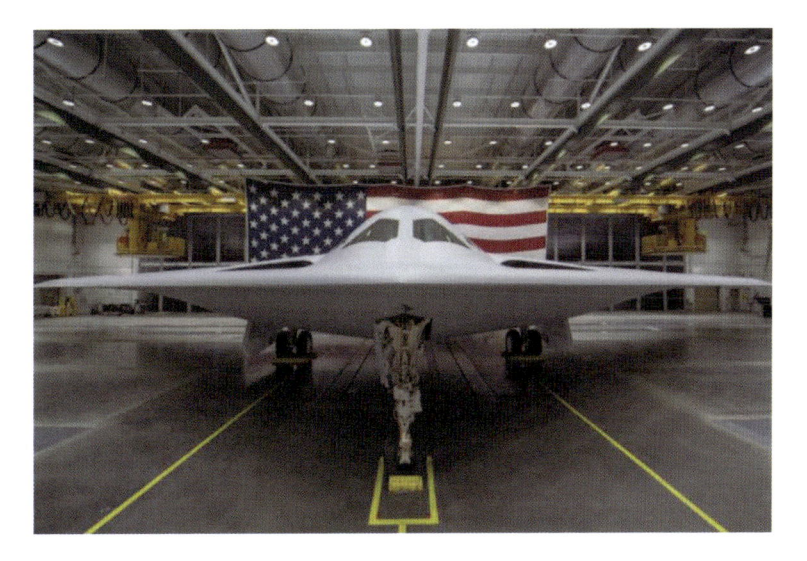

Unveiling of the Northrop Grumman B-21 Raider, December 2, 2022.
Credit: 94th Airlift Wing / Secretary of the Air Force Public Affairs

China and Russia are each also in the process of attempting to develop a modern stealth bomber. Following in the steps of the US, China has elected to pursue a 'flying wing' design, which is intrinsically more resistant to detection by low-bandwidth radar as used by large-spectrum ground stations, as well as by airborne radar systems such as those used with AWACS. Known as the H-20, the Chinese developmental stealth bomber has the turbofans of the aircraft imbedded in the upper surface of the aircraft's wings to reduce the infrared signature from below, similar to the B-2. The aircraft is expected to have a munitions payload of up to 23 tons, also in parallel with the Spirit. Projected to have a combat radius of approximately 5000 miles (8000 km), the H-20 in theory would be able to strike at targets out to and beyond the second island ring including Japan, the Philippines and Guam. The Russia stealth bomber under development is known as the PAK-DA. This aircraft is not as far along in its development at the Chinese aircraft or the B-21. Very little is known about the PAK-DA and it is likely that it remains in the early proto-typing stage, with even its shape not yet decided upon.

MODERN ATTACK HELICOPTERS

The other significant air arm that will be involved in any combat theatre are the attack helicopters. Where fixed wing aircraft are used to suppress command and control structures, radar facilities and airfields, rotary wing attack aircraft are specifically designed to engage and neutralize individual stationary and mobile targets. Fixed wing platforms such as fighters and bombers are typically operated by a nations air force, where helicopters are more often deployed by the army itself. Both the United States and Russia are leaders in the development of attack helicopters, with European nations and the Chinese also having produced examples of their own.

The premier attack helicopter to date remains the AH-64 Apache. With over 2400 units built, the twin-turboshaft attack helicopter is in service with the armies of the US, UK, Greece, Japan, Israel, the Netherlands, Singapore and the UAE. The Apache has seen extensive combat service including operations in Iraq, Afghanistan, Kosovo, Panama and Lebanon. First introduced to American forces in 1986 the AH-64 was designed to perform all-weather day and night missions and is equipped with enhanced optics, night vision, infrared cameras and radar. A tandem cockpit arrangement permits the rearward and upward positioned pilot to focus on flying the aircraft while the forward located weapons specialist focuses on threat and target identification. Though pilot and gunner have differentiated roles and responsibilities, each is able to perform all piloting and weapons aiming/launching functions if required. Armor plate between the pilot and gunner improves the probability that one of them would survive a strike on the aircraft. The airframe and quad-blade main rotor are designed to sustain 23 mm cannon fire. Four stub-wing pylon hardpoints carry ground attack missiles and rockets while a 30 mm (1.18) chaingun is mounted under the forward nose and aimed through the helmet motion of the pilot.

The Apache has undergone regular updates to upgrade its capabilities since its inception, the most significant being the introduction of the Longbow Apache. This version has a mast mounted radar which provides the ability to track and engage over 250 air and ground targets simultaneously to a range of 30 miles (50 km). Another addition was the Ground Fire Acquisition System, which detects ground fire directed toward the Apache and assists the aircraft crew with targeting and neutralizing these threats. The latest version of the Apache is known as the AH-64E Guardian. It is capable of remote controlling UAV's such as the RQ-7 Shadow or MQ-1C Grey Eagle, providing forward reconnaissance to better prepare themselves for a potential combat situation.

The AH-64E Apache Guardian Attack Helicopter
Credit: www.fairlifts.com

The Russian counterparts to the Apache are the Mi-28 Havoc (NATO reporting name) and the Ka-52 Alligator. Where the Mi-28 is used by the Russian Army, the Ka-52 is preferred for Special Forces operations. Like the Apache the Havoc is an all-weather, day-night, two seat helicopter designed specifically for the attack of armored units. Introduced in 2009, there have only been limited numbers built to date. The design is similar to the Apache, sharing the mounting of a 30 mm cannon under the aircraft nose and having a tandem stepped up cockpit which is armored to protect the crew. The pilot determines suitable air and lands targets using their helmet mounted display and hands these off to the navigator/weapons officer to engage. The weapons officer aims the aircrafts weapons through an integrated surveillance and fire control system. This offers them both wide and narrow optical viewers with a laser rangefinder.

The Mi-28 Havoc (left) and the Ka-52 Alligator (right)
Credit: sputniknews.com

The Ka-52 Alligator is a distinct aircraft, with two counter-rotating main rotors located coaxially. With production beginning in 2011, the dual side-by-side seat helicopter has only been built in small quantities. Side-by-side seating has been demonstrated to improve the ability of the pilot and weapons officers to co-ordinate their activities for both helicopters as well as fixed-wing aircraft. The dual main rotors give the aircraft superior aerodynamic performance as compared to conventionally designed helicopters with a tail rotor, providing the ability to perform loops, rolls and to strafe a target while circling about it. The Alligator is equipped with a day and night thermal imaging system and a dual radar able to detect and engage both aerial and ground targets.

The infrared unit consists of two spherical turrets with one mounted over the cockpit and the other under the nose. While the radar has a mast mounted unit for aerial targets and a nose-mounted unit for ground targets. A side-mounted cannon provides for fixed fire upon a target with more stability than a turret mounted gun and there are six pylon mounted hardpoints for attaching missiles and rocket launchers. The fire control system is able to share data with other aircraft and ground based systems, handing off and accepting targets between aircraft and ground stations. The Alligator is also equipped with an airborne defense system which offers improved protection against guided missiles. The system consists of radar warning receivers, laser warning receivers, MAW sensors, chaff and flare dispensers, ECM jammers and DIRCM jammers.

The Europeans have also developed their own dedicated attack helicopter, the Eurocopter Tiger. Having entered service in 2003 the Tiger is used by Germany, France and Spain, as well as by Australia. The Eurocopter is a multi-role attack helicopter suitable for reconnaissance, tank destroyer, close air support and helicopter escort missions. The day/night all-weather aircraft can operate from airbases as well as ships. Operated by a pilot in the front seating position of the tandem cockpit, the weapons officer sits to the rear, with both able to operate the flight controls and the weapons systems if necessary. The Tiger is of a composite construction which reduces its radar, visual, infrared and acoustic signatures compared to metallic helicopters. The stealth features, together with its high level of maneuverability, armored fuselage, system redundancy, radar and laser warning systems, missile approach detection systems and flare and chaff dispensers provide the Tiger excellent battlefield survivability.

The Tiger is also equipped with an extensive suite of modern avionics including a battlefield management system, satellite communications, automatic flight controls, dual mission control computers, GPS, helmet-mounted display, Doppler radar and FLIR sensor. Sensors are mounted at the front of the Tiger, around its periphery, and in a mast that is mounted above the blades. This Osiris mast-mounted sensor contains thermal/optical cameras and a laser range finger/tracker/designator. For weaponry there is a 30 mm Nexter turreted cannon and the helicopter can carry a wide range of rockets, air-to-air and air-to-surface missiles. When deploying missiles such as the Mistral, the Tiger can utilize the missiles off-boresight capability. The Tiger has seen service in Afghanistan, Libya and Mali, performing well in these theatres.

The Eurocopter Tiger
Credit: commons.wikimedia.org

AIR LAUNCHED WEAPONS

Fighter and bomber aircraft constitute a 'weapons delivery system', a means to transport and place a munition by air onto an intended target. But without munitions as sophisticated as the aircraft delivering them, then the odds of actually striking the target are low. Hundreds of bombers during WWII would drop many thousands of bombs towards targets while often missing them entirely. To compliment the development of modern aircraft, a plethora of corresponding advanced munitions have been developed to operate in concert with them. The American's lead in these efforts, with other nations often playing catch up or simply copying the American weapons form. There are some exceptions, where Russia has produced very novel and innovative weapons technologies based upon their own out-of-the-box thinking.

Airpower revolves around munitions that can attack stationary ground targets, mobile ground targets, other aircraft and shipping. Until the 1980's dumb bombs were primarily used to attack ground targets such as command structures, radar sites and bunkers. While unguided rockets were the choice for engaging mobile targets such as tanks, anti-aircraft guns and exposed infantry. Relatively poorly performing guided missiles were used to counter other aircraft. While larger missiles were employed to attack ships, along with the age-old techniques of dropping bombs and torpedoes. Each of these systems had a relatively low probability of actually striking their targets. Hitting a small target from an aircraft flying at a high altitude and zipping by at many hundreds of miles an hour is a notoriously challenging endeavour. Therefore those employing airpower to solve a dilemma often resorted to saturation techniques to neutralize a target. This typically resulted unfortunately in causing significant collateral damage to the surrounding area in the process.

The advent of computers with high processing speeds and large memory storage, along with an array of sensitive sensor technologies, allowed for the rapid development of precision guided munitions through the 1980's and 90's. And this momentum has only continued to accelerate over the last 20+ years. Precision weapons development has been a real game-changer, fundamentally altering the balance of power by restoring the advantage to the attacker. Precision munitions are able to accurately engage their targets over large distances through enhanced target acquisition and tracking technologies. While more advanced counter counter-measure abilities provide these weapons the capacity to avoid being jammed or spoofed. The result is that high cost systems and structures are now vulnerable to comparatively low cost weapons.

Precision Guided Bombs

The US was the first to develop air deployed precision guided ground attack munitions as the result of the perceived need for such weapons that arose during the Vietnam War. This was due to the high losses of aircraft that the American's suffered due to the anti-aircraft missiles provided to the Vietnamese by the Russians. US aircraft had to make repetitive attacks against the same targets because of the poor targeting ability of their free-falling bombs. Knowing that attacking aircraft would return to the same target to make another attempt to destroy it, the Vietnamese would concentrate their air defenses along the know attack corridors. The USAF realized that they needed bombs that could hit their targets precisely on the first attack run if they were to protect their pilots and aircraft.

The US was able to successfully employ the guided munitions they ultimately were to develop to effectively neutralize air defenses around Baghdad during the Persian Gulf War. It is estimated that the anti-aircraft defenses around Baghdad were about fourfold more intensive than those that had been around Saigon, and far more sophisticated. And yet through the use of precision munitions delivered by Stealth aircraft these defenses were destroyed without the loss of any aircraft. This was the first time that targets could be destroyed consistently, cost effectively and without causing significantly collateral damage by aircraft that were themselves essentially immune from counter-fire. Nations around the world watched and learned, and warfare technology was changed forever more.

The first precision-guided free-falling bombs, commonly referred to as 'smart-bombs', operated on the basis of laser-guidance. With the advent of the laser in the 1960's, the potential to use lasers for aiming bombs was quickly recognized. A laser designator functions by directing pulsed lasers at a target, known as 'illuminating' or 'painting' the target. The bombs themselves are equipped with a sensor able to detect the laser termination point, steerable fins and a small computer able to adjust the fins to direct the bomb toward the lased target. Initialled developed and fielded during the Vietnam War, smart bombs soon became accurate enough to be used to perform surgical strike missions. Gone were the days of saturating a target area with hundreds of bombs. A few bombs could now fulfill the mission objectives. Attacks by swarms of bombers or ground-attack aircraft unloading tons of munitions toward an intended target were replaced with a single aircraft loaded out with a precision strike package. Risk to pilots and their aircraft was reduced by minimising the number of aircraft required, while resulting collateral damage to civilian infrastructure became minimal.

The first laser-guided bomb was known as the BOLT-117. Introduced into service in 1968, the bomb was successfully used to damage bridges in North Vietnam that had otherwise proven resistant to conventional attacks. The BOLT quickly proved itself a reliable and accurate means to engage targets. More than 28,000 of these bombs would ultimately be dropped during the Vietnam War. A coded pulse was introduced into the laser illuminator, with the sensor on-board each bomb programmed to respond to only a certain pulse pattern. This avoided the munition being susceptible to counter-measures. If a continuous wave laser was employed then an opponent could re-direct the munition by generating a stronger laser illumination at a harmless location.

Based on the success of the BOLT during the Vietnam War, two families of laser-guided bombs were developed during the 1980's. These were known as Paveway II and Paveway III. Paveway II are 500 pound (230 kg) bombs and are used to attack vehicles and buildings. Paveway III are 2000 pounds (910 kg) and have a hardened nose section, specifically configured to penetrate and destroy large reinforced structures. These munitions saw their first wide-scale deployment during Operation Desert Storm, during which their proven precision capabilities fundamentally changed the nature of ground attack. Paveway II guidance was found to be so accurate that aircraft used the bomb to destroy moving tanks. While Paveway III bombs were used to destroy command and control bunkers, communication hubs and anti-aircraft missile installations.

Laser designation had a few intrinsic limitations however that became evident during Desert Storm. The attacking aircraft could only lase a target once quite close to it and then had to continue to fly straight toward the target following bomb release to maintain the illumination. This left the aircraft vulnerable to counter-fire. The system accuracy was also severely negatively impacted by bad weather and airborne dust. These weaknesses were overcome with the introduction of the Global Positioning System. GPS could provide a munition with guidance at both long range and under all weather conditions. Immediately upon releasing the munition the pilot could then leave the hostile area, take evasive maneuvers if required, or continue to engage additional targets.

The next step in smart bomb development was therefore to create GPS guidance kits. To avoid the high cost associated with producing dedicated munitions, kits were developed that could be directly attached to existing 'dumb' bombs. The Joint Direct Attack Munition (JDAM) is a GPS bomb guidance kit jointly developed by the USAF and USN - thus the 'joint' designation. First fielded in 1997, to date Boeing has assembled more than 430,000 JDAM kits for the USAF and USN. Able to be attached to bombs from 500 to 2000 pounds (230 to 910 kg), the cost of the average kit is $25,000 USD. Thereby JDAM provides a comparatively low cost, high accuracy method of delivery munitions. An aircraft loaded out with 16 JDAM equipped bombs no longer drops all of the bombs on one target. Rather, is drops one bomb on each of 16 targets.

A JDAM kit consists of three sections. There is a combined inertial guidance system/GPS guidance control kit, a body strake kit and a tail section which includes the aerodynamic control surfaces. These sections bolt onto the existing unguided gravity 'dumb' bombs. When the kit is attached to a bomb a GBU (Guided Bomb Unit) designation is assigned. The aircraft assigns the GBU with GPS attack coordinates prior to launch and then the guidance system alters the tail control surfaces to produce a free-fall path to the target. GPS also permits munition flight trajectory to be specified, permitting the launch aircraft to define the heading at which the munition approaches the target, as well at the angle of attack. Perpendicular attacks can be selected to maximize penetration on roof tops while oblique angles can be cued to penetrate through the weaker walls of buildings.

A GBU-31 GPS precision guided bomb, consisting of a regular Mk 84 dumb bomb fitted with a JDAM kit, pylon mounted under an aircraft wing
Credit: www.haf.gr

First deployed by B-2 Spirit stealth bombers during the Kosovo War, JDAM equipped bombs had a range of out to 17 miles (28 km) and an accuracy of better than within 23 feet (7 meters) of the intended point of impact. Released BGU's were found to strike their targets 87% of the time based upon more than 650 dropped units. To further improve their accuracy and to provide them the ability to even strike moving targets some JDAM's were also fitted with laser seekers. Laser JDAM's, or LJDAM, offered a dual seeker approach that proved highly successful throughout the Iraq War. Variants of the kit have also been developed with sensors that home in on radio emissions such as those produced by radar units, communication centers and electronic warfare jamming equipment.

Following development of JDAM, dedicated precision smart-bombs were also produced. The GBU-39 Small Diameter Bomb (SDB) is a 250 pound (110 kg) free-falling munition introduced in 2006 which is guided towards its target by GPS. The munition has a steel nosecone designed to penetrate hardened targets and a 137 pound (62 kg) blast fragmentation warhead. The SDB is a 'glide-bomb', onto which small folding wings have been added to provide an extended range. This range is 65 miles (110 km) against stationary targets and 45 miles (72 km) against moving targets when launched from maximum altitude. Upon approaching the target a terminal homing guidance package is activated. The tri-mode seeker includes laser guidance, infrared homing and millimeter wave active radar homing. Together these give the munition an accuracy to within 3 feet (1 meter). The SBD will penetrate more than 1 meter of reinforced concrete as well as the roof armor of any armored vehicle.

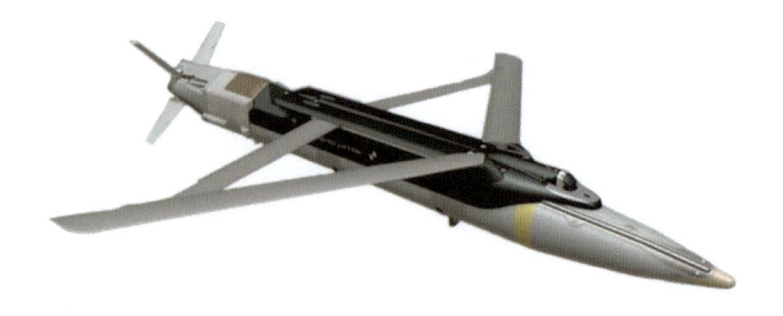

GBU-39 Small Diameter Bomb with folding wings in deployed position
Credit: www.shephardmedia.com

Another excellent example of a guided glide-bomb is the AGM-154 Joint Standoff Weapon (JSOW). Developed jointly by the USAF and USN, the precision guided 1000 pound (490 kg) glide bomb was introduced into service in 1998. JSOW appears in size and shape similar to a cruise missile but it is unpowered. Using folding wings as a means to 'glide' and thereby extend its range, the AGM-154 is able to strike targets out to a distance of 80 miles (130 km) from its high altitude release point. The munition was specifically designed so that aircraft could release an all-weather fire-and-forget precision guided unpowered munition at beyond typical anti-aircraft weapons range. The JSOW offers a common munitions carrying air vehicle, referred to as a 'truck', which contains and releases the munition, similar in this regard to a cruise missile. This makes the JSOW a very versatile yet comparatively inexpensive delivery system.

Aircrew loading a JSOW onto an aircraft pylon
http://military-tech-equipment.blogspot.com

There are currently two version to the bomb available, the AGM-154A and the 154C. The A version distributes combined effects bomblets and sells for $282,000 USD, while the C version has a multi-stage warhead and sells for $719,000 USD. The A version is guided by satellite/inertial navigation while the C version adds a terminal infrared homing seeker. The AGM-154A truck contains 145 BLU-97/B Combined Effects Bomb sub-munitions. These bomblets contain shaped charge warheads along with fragmentation and incendiary components. The JSOW seeds the designated area with these bomblets, which then impact armored targets and structures, sowing destruction along their path. The AGM-154C truck by contrast contains a single dual stage 500 pound (225 kg) warhead designed to penetrate thick hardened structures. The first warhead penetrates the structure, permitting the second warhead to enter the structure and detonate within it. There was also a B version which distributed 24 infrared homing shaped charged warheads designed for top-down attack of armored units, but this version was never procured. While it would offer higher precision attacks on armored vehicles than the A version, the smaller number of sub-munitions and the greater cost per unit resulted in its cancellation.

Computer model of the JSOW showing wings in deployed position.
Credit: turbosquid.com

The JSOW was first employed during the Iraq War to suppress enemy air defenses. AGM-154A's were launched from carrier-based F/A-18C's, saturating anti-aircraft positions with the highly destructive bomblets. With over

400 JSOW's launched throughout the Iraq War, the munition successfully demonstrated its effectiveness in neutralizing hostile targets at range. Since the Iraq War the highly adaptable JSOW has regularly received upgrades such as anti-GPS jamming capabilities and is being evaluated for other payload configurations. In addition to being used by the USAF and USN, JSOW is also employed by Poland, Turkey, Netherlands, Saudi Arabia, Canada, Finland, Greece, Australia, UAE, Singapore and Taiwan.

Since their introduction by the American's, other nations have developed their own version of air deployed smart-bombs. The French Armement Air-Sol Modulaire (Air-to-Ground Modular Weapon) or AASM is a guidance kit similar to JDAM that attaches to a dumb bomb and converts it into a precision guided munition. The munition is guided by GPS/inertial navigation and infrared homing, giving it an accuracy of better than 39 inches (1 meter). Having entered service with the French Airforce and Navy in 2007, the guidance kit is also used by Morocco, Egypt, Qatar and India. Similar guidance kits include the Sudarshan and the Griffin, developed by India and Israel respectively. Russia has developed their own smart munitions as well. The Russian KAB-500KR is a 1100 pound (500 kg) electro-optical TV-guided fire and forget bomb. It uses a low-light television seeker along with guidance fins to turn a general purpose dumb bomb into a guided unpowered glide bomb. Since its inception, various upgrade options have been introduced. The KAB-500S-E is equipped with satellite guidance to provide all-weather capabilities. It utilizes the Russian equivalent of GPS for guidance, known as GLONASS.

Russian KAB-500 laser guided smart-bomb
Credit: the48ers.com

Anti-Tank Guided Missiles (ATGM's)

Air launched 'fire and forget' anti-tank guided missiles (ATGM) were developed in parallel with those used by ground units. Air launch systems however tend to be larger and more sophisticated. The first of these deployed in large numbers is the American Hellfire. A third generation ground attack missile introduced into service in 1982, it can be used to engage a broad range of ground targets. It provides aircraft such as the Boeing AH-64 Apache helicopter gunship with a significant capability as a 'tank-buster'. The Apache is able to carry up to 16 of these missiles and it was used to good effect in destroying Saddam's armor units during both the Persian Gulf War and the Iraq War. The

Hellfire is also the primary ground strike capable missile used on American Unmanned Air Vehicles (UAV) such as the General Atomics MQ-1 Predator, which will be discussed in a later chapter. The Hellfire is used by the US along with many of its allies and has seen extensive combat engagement in multiple operations including Operation Desert Storm, Operation Enduring Freedom and Operation Iraqi Freedom.

The original Hellfire missile employs laser guidance, with the missile homing in on the reflection of a laser designator directed toward the target. The source of the designator may be either from the launch platform (i.e., the aircraft firing the missile) or from an independent source, such as infantry stationed in the area of the threat. This later arrangement not only permits the launch platform to fire multiple missiles at multiple targets near simultaneously, but it also allows the launch platform to take evasive maneuvers following missile launch in hostile environments. The use of an independent laser designator source also permits non-line-of-sight (NLOS) engagements in which the missile needs to be merely launched in the direction of the intended target. Once the lased target is detected by the missile it with then automatically adjust its course as required.

Hellfire's mounted onto stub wing pylons of an Apache
Credit: activistpost.com

In the early 1990's the modular designed Hellfire II was introduced. This system permits the guidance system and warhead type to be tailored to the needs of a specific operation. Warhead options available include the standard High Explosive Anti-Tank (HEAT) warhead, blast fragmentation sleeve warhead and metal augmented charge (MAC). MAC is more commonly known as a thermobaric warhead, a weapon type that generates extremely high temperatures and pressures at the target. Thermobaric weapons are very effective when used to penetrate and destroy hardened structures. Guidance system selection options include the standard laser designator or a millimetric wave (mmW) radar. mmW guidance involves mounting a radar transmitter/seeker into the head of the missile. The target is pre-selected by the aircraft weapons officer. Following launch the missile then automatically homes in on the identified target without any further instructions from the launch platform. It can be used for either a Line-of-Sight (LOS) or Non-Line-of-Sight (NLOS) attack profile and is not impeded by adverse weather conditions or obscuration smoke.

Some controversy has arisen regarding use of AGM-114's launched from UAV's operated by Intelligence Agencies to eliminate high-value individual targets (i.e., air launched targeted assassination). This approach however has proven extremely successful in suppressing many terrorist organizations around the globe and therefore its utilization in this role is not likely to cease. One variant of the Hellfire used in this application is the AGM-114R9X, which makes use of blades rather than a traditional explosive warhead. Six swing-out blades with a diameter of 3.5 feet (1.1 meter) cut through the target area. This permits surgical strikes yet minimizes the occurrence of collateral damage that otherwise may occur with explosive charges. Another version simply conceals a 100 pound (45 kg) mass of steel within its body and destroys its target through sheer momentum and energy transfer effects, again limiting collateral damage.

The Maverick air-to-ground tactical missile is similar to the Hellfire, but much larger. It is a multi-functional precision-guided missile that can be used to engage a wide range of targets including tanks and other mobile platforms, buildings and other hardened structures and even ships. The Maverick measures 8 feet (2.4 m) in length and 12 inches in diameter (30 cm) in diameter, has long-chord delta wings, can engage targets 16 miles (25 km) from the launch point, travels at 620 miles per hour (1150 km/hr), and weighs between 362 pounds (210 kg) and 675 pounds (306 kg), depending on the variant. In active service since 1972, tens of thousands of the missile have been fabricated, exported to over 30 countries and seen wide deployment in many conflicts including the Vietnam War, Yom Kippur War, Iran-Iraq War and Persian Gulf War, and Iraq War.

The Maverick has seen multiple revisions to both the warhead and the guidance system since its inception. Warhead options include a 126 lb (57 kg) shaped charge warhead with a contact fuze mounted to the nose and a 300 lb (136 kg) penetrating blast fragmentation warhead with a delayed-action fuze. The former warhead is effective against armored units while the second is effective as a bunker buster, in which the hardened missile penetrates the target before detonating. Guidance system options available include laser designator seeker, infrared seeker, electro-optical (TV camera mounted in nose), and charge-coupled device (optical with 3x sensitivity of electro-optical system). The target is selected by the pilot of the aircraft launching the missile and following launch the Maverick homes in on the target without any further input required by the launch platform.

The Hellfire's larger cousin, the Maverick
Credit: military.com

The Europeans have also developed some great air-launched anti-tank guided missiles (ATGM). The British Brimstone is an example of a third-generation fire-and-forget air-launched ATGM that entered service in 2005. The missile guidance system is a dual laser and millimetric wave (mmW) active radar homing seeker. With a tandem shaped charge warhead the missile is suitable for engaging armored vehicles protected with Explosive Reactive Armor (ERA), such as is typically used by the Russians. The missile is equipped with sufficient computational and sensor capabilities to enable it to independently identify suitable targets to engage and to determine the optimal location on the target to strike to maximize delivered damage. When multiple Brimstones are launched toward a set of targets and in the event that multiple Brimstone's happened to select the same target to attack, then the remaining missiles will automatically reacquire and select another target to attack in the event of the original target being destroyed by one of the missiles. The Brimstone saw extensive use during the Afghanistan War and demonstrated a success rate of greater than 90% in striking the intended target.

Brimstone missiles mounted on a wing pylon below an aircraft wing
Credit: quwa.org

Israel has developed their own sophisticated ATGM as well, known as the Nimrod. The long-range missile can also be used to engage hardened infantry structures along with naval craft. Guided through a semi-active laser guidance system in which a target is identified with a laser designator from a distance of up to up 16 miles (26 km), the missile uses a laser homing seeker to guide its flight toward the target. Initially flying high above the ground the missile rapidly descends upon approach to the target at a 45 degree angle, seeking to strike armored assets on their more vulnerable upper surface. The Nimrod is a large and heavy missile weighting 330 lbs (150 kg) together with its launch tube and has a substantial powerful warhead which weighs 31 lbs (14 kgs).

Air-to-Air Missiles

Air-to-air guided missiles were developed along with the fighter jet after World War II to provide aircraft a means to engage one another other than using machine-guns and cannon. The resulting missiles are typically described by their range, which then determines their intended purpose. Short-range missiles are used against other fighters during dog-fights. They typically rely on heat seeking warheads for guidance and are used within visual range of the target. Medium-range missiles are used to engage an enemy beyond visual range and usually rely on radar for guidance. While long-range missiles are meant to be used to engage large aircraft that are slow to respond such as bombers, transports, AWACS, surveillance and re-fueling aircraft. Missiles are often launched in pairs. While an opponent may be able to take evasive maneuvers and avoid being hit by the first incoming missile, this action will cause the opponent to become distracted as well as to lose critical speed, rendering them more vulnerable to the second missile.

First generation anti-aircraft missiles actually had a low probability of striking their target and early fighter jets still relied heavily upon the use of cannon fire to engage their opponent once their missile attacks upon one another failed to produce results. Maneuvering to avoid one another's missiles however usually resulted in each aircraft having lost any original advantage they had in air speed, altitude and position. And therefore a good old fashion close-range gun based dog fight ensued – often referred to as a knife fight in a phone booth. But the odds of success when deploying air-to-air missiles continuously improved as the sensor and computer technologies were enhanced. Air deployed anti-aircraft missiles are now consistently deadly enough that the first to detect an opponent and launch a missile or pair of missiles at them is typically the one to win the fight. This is the reason that stealth is so important now – a pilot needs to be the first to identify their opponent and fire upon them if they wish to see tomorrow.

The most ubiquitous of all aircraft deployed anti-aircraft missiles is the American Sidewinder. The AIM-9 Sidewinder is a visual range 'fire-and-forget' heat seeking air-to-air missile that has been in US inventories in various configuration since the 1950's. More than 110,000 AIM-9 missiles have been produced by the US and other nations, making it the most widely produced and used Western air-to-air missile. Regular upgrades to the missile have occurred since its inception, with the latest version of the missile, the AIM-9X, having entered service in 2003 at a unit price of $472,000 USD.

The AIM-9X has a range of 12 miles (20 km) and tracks its target by homing in on the infrared signature the target emits, particularly from the jet exit nozzle. Equipped with a 20.8 pound (9.4 kg) WDU-17/B annular blast-fragmentation warhead the IR proximity fuse causes the missile to detonate on impact with a target or at its closest approach to the target. Weighing 188 pounds (85 kg), the AIM-9X is 9 feet 11 inches in length (3 meters) with a diameter of 5 inches (127 mm). It is propelled by a Hercules/Bermite Mk. 36 solid-fuel rocket which accelerates the missile to approximately Mach 2.5 beyond the speed of the launch platform.

The AIM-9X Sidewinder missile offers several enhancements to prior versions. Most significantly, the targeting systems for the missile has been directly integrated into the pilot's helmet. Known as the Joint Helmet Mounted Cueing System, it gives the pilot the ability to aim the missile simply through looking toward the intended target. The infrared sensor arc was also increased, permitting the missile to identify and track targets that are not in line with the flight direction of the firing aircraft. This was achieved through inclusion of an imaging infrared focal plane array (FPA) which provides for 90° off-boresight targeting capabilities. The AIM-9X was also upgraded with an improved ability to resist jamming and a 3D thrust-vectoring control (TVC) system was added. This provides for the ability to perform tight turns, further facilitating off-boresight engagements.

F-16 launching a AIM-9X
Credit: militaryleak.com

The counterpart to the Sidewinder is the medium range AIM-120 AMRAAM. The AMRAAM fire-and-forget all weather day/night air-to-air missile has been in service with the USAF and USN since 1991 at a unit cost of $1.1 million USD. The AMRAAM tracks its target through an active transmit-receive radar guidance system. Weighing 335 lbs (152 kg) it is 12 feet in length (3.7 meters) and is powered by a solid-fuel rocket motor that propels the missile to a maximum speed of Mach 4. The AMRAAM is armed with a 40 pound (18 kg) WDU-41/B high explosive blast-fragmentation warhead. Similar to the Sidewinder, the AMRAAM also continuously receives new upgrades to enhance its capabilities.

The latest version is the AIM-120D. The missile has a 50% extended effective combat range to 100 miles (160 km) and the missiles active transmit radar guidance also has an extended range, increased sensitivity and a wider arc of engagement. The AMRAAM can also be launched toward a target beyond the range of its own radar and guided toward a known target through a two-way data link. This link is resistant to jamming and hacking and provides radar data to the missile from either the launch aircraft or an AWAC station. The AMRAAM acquires lock-on once the target comes within range of the missiles internal radar. AIM-120D also includes a GPS system for improved navigation.

Comparison of size and appearance of AIM-9X and AMRAAM
Credit: defense-studies.blogspot.com

When the AMRAMM was developed, it offered significantly greater capabilities than air-to-air missiles produced by China or Russia at that time. These nations however have made significant progress in advancing their own air-to-air missile technology in recent years, especially with regards to range. Therefore the AMRAAM is slated to be supplemented by the long range AIM-260 Joint Air Tactical Missile (JATM) starting in 2024. The AIM-260 must have the same dimensions as the AIM-120 to be able to fit within the weapons bays of the F-22 and F-35. Therefore the additional range will be achieved by using a more powerful rocket fuel. In addition to extended range, a number of additional features have been introduced to the missile to further enhance its capabilities.

The AIM-260 is equipped with a dual mode seeker which utilizes both radar and infrared target acquisition and tracking capabilities. This combination of tracking methods increases the missile's ability to home in on its target. The dual mode seeker also enhances the AIM-260's resistance to being jammed by electronic warfare countermeasures. This is necessary as there is a concern that the AIM-120 is vulnerable to modern day digital radio frequency memory (DRFM) jamming techniques employed by both China and Russia. The JATM also includes an encrypted two-way data link. This system permits secure communications between the missile once in flight and the aircraft from which his was launched. The aircraft can provide information from its own larger radar unit to the missile to facilitate its homing in on the intended target, or to re-assign the missile to another target during flight.

Europeans also have developed their own advanced air-to-air missiles. The Meteor is a medium range missile developed by the UK. Guided by an active radar the missile has a range in excess of 90 miles (150 km). It is powered by a solid-fuel ramjet motor, cruises at a speed of Mach 4 and has the ability to rapidly accelerate once it has lock-on to a target. Multiple sensors are used to determine the optimal point of detonation of the blast-fragmentation warhead. The missile is resistant to a heavy electronic countermeasures (ECM) environment and a two-way datalink permits mid-course retargeting. The missile is used by the UK, Sweden, Germany, Spain, France and Italy.

A meteor air-to-air missile shown next to a F-35
Credit: blogs.plymouth.ac.uk

The Russians of course also have various air-to-air missiles in their inventories. Their most recent and advanced of these is known as the Vympel R-37M. Introduced into service in 2019 and given the NATO designation AA-13 Axehead, it has a weight of 1320 pounds (600 kg), is 13 feet 9 inches long (4.2 meters), 15 inches in diameter (38 cm) and armed with a 135 pound (60 kg) high explosive fragmentation warhead. It is propelled by a boost-sustain solid rocket that gives it a travel speed of Mach 5 and a range of 90 miles (150 km) for a direct shot and 240 miles (400 km) for a cruise glide profile. Guidance systems include inertial, semi-active and active radar. It is a large long-range missile comparable to the American AIM-54 Phoenix and is intended to target low maneuverability strategic air assets such as bombers, fuel tankers and reconnaissance aircraft. The missiles very long range permits the launch aircraft to fire the weapon while out of range of defensive aircraft.

The large Vympel R-37M (grey missile) loaded onto an underwing pylon of a Su-35
Credit: armasrusasb.blogspot.com

The Chinese have recently made significant strides in their air-to-air missile development. In fact the AIM-260 was created specifically to counter recently developed Chinese missiles with ranges that supposedly surpass similar missile in American and European inventories. The basic design of all Western air-to-air missiles were created many years ago, with upgrades simply building onto these existing frames. Being late contenders, the Chinese sought specifically to create a new generation of missiles with features that exceed existing Western capabilities. Therefore the design of their new air-to-air missiles stressed high velocity, long range and inherent jam resistant technologies.

The most impressive recent Chinese air-to-air missiles are the PL-10 and the PL-15. The PL-10 is a Chinese short-range missile with infrared guidance similar in design to the Sidewinder. The PL-10 has a wide arc of detection for off-boresight targeting, able to be fired upon targets up to 90 degrees out of alignment with the launch aircraft. When fired from the J-20 aircraft, the PL-10 is aimed and fired using the Helmet Mounted Display (HMD), similar to modern Western aircraft. The missile also has embedded anti-jamming technology. The PL-10 is claimed to have a range greater than that of the AIM-9X, though the validity of this claim has never been demonstrated. The missile may in fact have a long range, but lack the ability to effectively strike the target.

The PL-15 is a Chinese long range air-to-air missile comparable to the American AMRAAM, directed toward its target by an active electronically scanned radar.

Powered by a pulsed solid-propellant rocket the missile travels at a speed of between Mach 4 and Mach 5. The missile is claimed to have an operational range of between 120 and 180 miles (200 and 300 km). If true this would give it almost twice the range of an AIM-102D AMRAAM. Having entered service with the Chinese Airforce in 2016, it is carried by the Chengdu J-10C, Shenyang J-16 and the Chengdu J-20 aircraft. The 13 foot (4 meter) long missile also has anti-jamming features integrated into the missile.

PL-10 (left) and PL-15 (right) air-to-air missiles mounted on wing pylons of a Chinese J-10, also visible in the background. The J-10 can be considered as a poor Chinese copy of the American F-16.
Credit: thedrive.com

One thing to always keep in mind is that while Chinese missile capabilities appear on paper to have surpassed

Western equipment, the validity of this claim by the Chinese is yet to be determined. While the missiles are of a newer design and incorporate many sophisticated features, the proper functionality of complex systems is often only achieved following significant combat experience and corrective iterations to work out the bugs. Western technology in general, and American specifically, has incorporated a long history of experience into their designs and actual combat effectiveness is well known. This is not the case for Chinese equipment that lacks any actual combat experience to gauge real-life performance.

As well it should be remembered that Western nations tend to publicly state the minimum capabilities of their equipment, not wishing to provide potential opponents with a clear understanding of their capabilities. Russians and Chinese by contrast, trying to both build a reputation as re-emerging powers as well as to promote potential international arms sales, tend to over-exaggerate claims regarding their equipment performance, claims which cannot be independently validated. So for example, the PL-15 might be able to fly for 180 miles (300 km) before striking the ground, but this is not how Western nations would measure a missiles maximum effective range.

Cruise Missiles

Cruise missiles had their origin during World War II, when Germany developed the V-1 'flying bomb'. Cruise missiles are essentially self-navigating flying munitions that can be used to strike land or sea targets. Some types are air launched, while others can be launched from land-based launch sites or from ships. Typically powered by jet engines, some also include an initial short burst rocket to assist in achieving a high starting velocity. All take advantage of the lift generated by the inclusion of small wings. Some fly at their target from high up and then descend steeply upon their target upon terminal approach. Other's skim over trees or the water surface to avoid detection by radar. America has been a leader in this field for many years and the precision of their cruise missiles was demonstrated decisively during both the Persian Gulf and Iraq Wars. China and Russia have also recently created their own advanced cruise missiles. The goal for each of these nation is to try to create cruise missiles able to penetrate through the highly effective anti-missile defense systems of America and European nations. Therefore both China and Russia claim that the speed and maneuverability of their cruise missiles exceeds that of many existing Western counterparts, which were designed before the development of modern air defense systems. But of course assertions of superior performance by China and Russia are stated without being supported by hard evidence. In general it was found that the performance of cruise missiles used by Russia during their invasion of Ukraine was disappointing.

On display at a museum, a German WWII V-1 jet powered 'flying bomb', the first mass produced cruise missile
Credit: flickr.com

One of the premier air-launched cruise missiles available is the American AGM-158 Joint Air-to Surface Standoff Missile (JASSM). It is a low observable standoff ground attack munition developed through a joint effort by the USAF and the USN. Airforce versions of the AGM-158 can be launched from both bombers and fighters while the Navy's version is meant to be launched from the F-35B. The JASSM has a stealthy configuration with a low RCS to render it challenging for an opponent to detect at long range or to accurately track at short range. The baseline AGM-158A entered service in 2009 at a unit cost of $1.27 million USD. The cruise missile weighs 2250 pounds (1021 kg), is 14 feet (2.4 meters) long and is powered by a turbojet engine. Equipped with a 1000 pound (454 kg) penetrating warhead the missile has a range of 230 miles (370 km). The missile is designed to be air launched against blast resistant land structure such as bunkers and command and control centers. Along with the USAF, the missile is also used by Australia, Finland and Poland.

JASSM being launched from an F-16, along with an image of how the AGM-154 appears once its wings are deployed.
Credit: aerospacemanufacturinganddesign.com

Upon being launched, folded wings embedded within the AGM-158 are deployed outward and the turbojet is activated. During its flight time the missile constantly transmits its location and status back to the launch platform through a data link. The JASSM employs a number of concurrent guidance systems to guide itself toward and precisely onto its intended target. GPS is used to guide the missile to the target area, where an inertial navigation system (INS) is used to collate with the GPS, as well as to provide a back-up if the GPS signal were to be jammed.

Once the target area is approached then an infrared homing sensor is activated. This system is capable of automatic target recognition and guides the munition toward the target during the terminal stage of its flight. Successful impact of the missile with its target is confirmed through the last data linked transmission of its position back to the launch platform.

The turbojet engine of the JASSM propels it to only subsonic speeds, as is the case with most US cruise missiles. Where supersonic or even hypersonic speeds might be considered preferable, achieving such speeds comes as a huge cost both in terms of increased price per missile as well as reduced missile range. Note that if a missile travels faster with the same amount of on-board fuel, then the range is correspondingly reduced. To achieve the same range, a faster moving missile would have to be much larger and more complicated, driving up cost as well as limiting potential launch platforms. Therefore the US and Western nations in general tend to build subsonic missiles, as these are capable of penetrating existing Russian and Chinese defenses to achieve a target strike. The resulting low cost per unit permits many of these relatively inexpensive missiles to be built for a given amount of funding.

Since its original inception, other variants of the AGM-158 have been developed. The AGM-158B JASSM-ER (Extended Range) entered service in 2014 and has a range of approximately 575 miles (925 km). While the AGM-158C is a JASSM-ER reconfigured as a Long Range Anti-Shipping Missile (LRASM) with an alternate seeker head. It can be launched by both USAF and USN aircraft. The surface skimming missile is capable of autonomous navigation, being able to move around opponents that are not the intended target. The latest addition to the family, the AGM-158D JASSM-XR (eXtreme Range), has a further extended range out to 1200 miles (1900 km). The additional range was largely achieved simply through a wing re-design. At a unit cost of $1.5 million USD the missile also incorporates an upgraded missile control unit and a secure GPS receiver. Larger than the previous versions, The AGM-158D weighs 5000 pounds (2300 kg) and has a 2000 pound (910 kg) warhead. Greater ranges for new or modified cruise missiles are introduced to permit the launch aircraft to remain beyond the radii of the ever expanding perimeter of similarly evolving air defense systems – an endless game of cat and mouse.

The Russians also have air-launched cruise missiles within their inventories. The Kh-59M Ovod, NATO designation AS-13 Kingbolt, is an air launched anti-shipping cruise missile that has been in service with Russia since the 1980's, receiving regular upgrades and enhancements. The missile weighs 2050 pounds (930 kg) and is armed with either a cluster or shaped charge fragmentation warhead which weighs 705 pounds (320 kg). The missile is powered by a combined rocket booster and turbojet, attaining speeds upwards of Mach 0.80. The missile is guided by INS during regular flight toward a pre-programmed location, approaching its target at only 23 feet (7 meters) above the surface of the sea. At 6 miles (10 km) from the target the missile then engages a TV guidance for the terminal phase of the approach. An operator on the aircraft can view the image in the camera and selects the target for the missile to attack.

The requirement for manual selection of the target for the Kingbolt renders the missile vulnerable to being jammed as the radio signal to and from the missile to the launch aircraft can be interrupted. Also an attack on the launch aircraft by another aircraft can disturb the operator from performing this function. To remove this limitation, the most modern versions are equipped with either an infrared or active radar seeker than provides the missile with the ability to select its own target if there is no human selection received. A low RCS version has also been developed as well as land attack versions. With a maximum range of 340 miles (550 km), the missile can be launched at a range beyond that for which most available air defense weapons could counter-attack the launch platform. However, if deployed while attacking a carrier group, there might very well be opposing attack aircraft in the vicinity. Russia sells the Kingbolt on the international arms market, will sales made to both China and India.

AS-13 Kingbolt launched from a Su-30MK Flanker. The rocket assist can be seen below the missile.
Credit: navyrecognition.com

Anti-Aircraft / Anti-Missile Systems

As we have seen, through the later half of the 20th century aircraft transitioned from attacking one another with machine-guns and cannon to firing upon each other with heat seeking and radar guided missiles. Ships no longer fired line-of-sight shells with a maximum range of 20 miles (32 km) at one another but began to launch cruise missiles with ranges of many hundreds of miles and possessing their own guidance and targeting systems. Then cruise missiles evolved so that they could be deployed from subs. Ballistic missiles and cruise missiles, launched by land, sea or air, became able to accurately strike strategically important targets such as airfields and communication centers deep behind enemy lines. Long range ground and sea launched anti-aircraft missiles replaced anti-aircraft cannon, providing far greater range and accuracy. While ground attack aircraft replaced their free-falling unguided bombs with guided glide bombs and precision guided missiles to increase the range at which they could accurately launch their weapons and thus reduce their own vulnerability.

Military organizations around the world first became fully aware of the significant impact that the development of these new guided missile systems would have upon their structure and tactics as a result of the American involvement in Vietnam. The Americans had designed numerous fast-moving tactical ground attack aircraft that they knew would be challenging for the archaic air defense systems employed by North Vietnamese forces to engage. The Soviets however had provided the North Vietnamese with their latest ground launched SA-2 high altitude anti-aircraft missile system. These missiles were used to good effect against US aircraft and the USAF was stunned by both the range and accuracy of the SA-2. Despite their efforts to neutralize the missiles effectiveness using chaff, electronic counter-measures, defensive maneuvering and the employment of anti-radar missiles, SA-2's would ultimately claim the destruction of hundreds of American ground attack aircraft as well as B-52 Stratofortress's throughout the duration of the war.

Traditional projectiles fired from ship cannon, artillery pieces and anti-aircraft guns had a low individual probability of striking their target. Military tactics against an opponent armed with such guns was therefore simply to push through to the target, accepting the low rate of incurred losses in the process. But the advent of guided missiles fundamentally changed the nature of combat by introducing a near one shot-one kill weapon system. Military tactics and defensive systems would have to be modified to account for this new factor of war. The world's militaries frantically began to invest in methods able to counter the missile systems that they had only recently developed. Passive approaches such as stealth, jammers and decoys were investigated and developed into functional technologies. Some nations also began to attempt to enhance the guidance and targeting systems of their existing gun and missile systems to the point that they would be able to intercept incoming missile threats.

Launch of a SA-2 anti-aircraft missile during the Vietnam War
Credit: vietnampathfinder.com

At first it was doubted that weapons could ever be created that would be able to react fast enough or be maneuverable enough to counter rapidly approaching missiles. The challenge in developing an effective anti-missile system was in performing all of the related tasks very precisely and quickly. These included detecting a missile launch, tracking the incoming missile, predicting its flight path to determine whether the missile was a threat, accurately identifying the exact location of the missile, linking this information to the anti-missile launch system, calculating an intercept launch path between the incoming missile and the counter-munition, and lastly accurately launching the counter-munition. Being able to perform all of these steps would require the highly synchronized interaction of a range of sophisticated sensors and networked computer systems.

The challenges associated with developing an effective missile defense system were overcome however with the advent of compact computers, which provided for the required processing capabilities and system response times. By the 1980's ships were being equipped with gun and missile systems which in theory, as demonstrated through testing, could engage incoming missile threats. The first successful defeat of an actual incoming missile threat by an anti-missile system occurred in 1991 during the Persian Gulf War. Iraq had fired a Silkworm cruise missile at the USS Missouri of the USN. The HMS Gloucester of the UK was serving as a defensive missile cruiser for the joint task force and identified the incoming threat. The Gloucester launched a Seat Dart missile at the cruise missile in response and destroyed the incoming threat. This success guaranteed the commitment by military forces of the world to the further development and deployment of anti-missile systems.

While these first early missile defense systems performed relatively well, modern systems are far more capable. They are able to counter a range of missile threats, from sea-skimming anti-shipping cruise missiles to high altitude ballistic missiles. Modern systems are also able to track and counter waves of incoming threats to deal with saturation attack tactics. These systems are also typically layered, consisting of both long-range and short-range anti-missile launchers and munitions. The systems are capable of detecting whether the long-range counter-munitions were successful in defeating the incoming threats and if not, will automatically prepare the secondary close-support weapon to engage those remaining. The successful development of missile defense systems was critical to ensuring that military forces were not mere sitting ducks to missile attacks but were able to continue to pursue their missions with the assurance that they would be able to contend with the opponents response.

Close-in-Weapon Systems

Close-in-Weapon System (CIWS) is the term used to describe the Active Protection Systems used on Naval vessels. CIWS are point-defense weapons that are capable of engaging incoming threats at short ranges. They are able to provide protection to the ship against approaching anti-shipping cruise missiles, anti-radar missiles and guided bombs, as well as against low flying aircraft and approaching small surface vessels. All ships of an even reasonably modern navy will be equipped with CIWS protection. CIWS has evolved such that they are now also often installed at military bases to protect them from incoming threats. When part of a layered anti-missile defense strategy, CIWS constitute the last line of defense for the system.

CIWS are classified as either gun-based or missile-based. In each case a detection radar identifies an incoming missile threat and then a targeting radar provides a lock-on to the threat. The radar data is processed by a central computer that outputs a firing solution to the CIWS counter-measure launch system. For a gun-based system this consists of a rotary cannon, typically mounted on a traversable gimbal assembly. The computer provides directional data to the cannon which then dispels a huge number of metal slugs toward the threat. For a missile-based system, both range and directional data are provided to the launch system. A rapidly accelerating missile with an explosive warhead is then launched toward the target. The anti-missile missile independently tracks the incoming target, either through an infrared sensor, active radar or passive radar. This permits the missile to make course corrections to compensate for defensive maneuvers taken by the incoming threat. The missile then detonates its warhead at the point of closest approach to the threat.

The first operational CIWS was the American Phalanx. In service since the 1980's, upgraded versions of the system continue to protect American and allied ships of 15 other nations, including the UK, Australia and Canada. Utilizing a multi-barrel 20 mm M61 Vulcan Gatling autocannon, targets are identified and tracked by a fire control radar system. The pivoting cannon is oriented toward an incoming target and unleashes depleted uranium or tungsten shells toward the target upon its terminal approach toward the ship. This denies the incoming threat any time to react to the wall of metal suddenly between it and the ship. Slamming into the wall of metal the threat is ripped apart and disintegrates. The system is effective against a broad range of incoming anti-shipping missiles including both maneuvering sea-skimmers and high AOA missiles that descend rapidly downward onto their intended target. The Phalanx, like other CIWS, is a fully autonomous system. The time available to react to an incoming threat is so brief that a person in-the-loop would only hinder operation of the system. As the earliest functional CIWS, the Phalanx therefore can be considered to be the first fully autonomous lethal robot.

A Phalanx CIWS in operation firing rounds through the rotary cannon
Credit: asdnews.com

Similar to other gun-based CIWS the Phalanx is a close-range defensive system, engaging incoming threats at a maximum distance of about 1600 yards (1500 meters) from the ship. Despite this limited range, the Phalanx has proven itself to be highly reliable in providing effective missile defense. They are also relatively inexpensive to both procure and operate as compared with missile-based defense systems. Larger US naval ships will typically employ a layered missile defense approach which will include longer range missile systems along with multiple Phalanx. While smaller US naval ships will tend to rely solely upon the Phalanx to provide a defense response. Storing 1500 rounds of ammunition and firing approximately 100 rounds at each target, a single Phalanx can defend a ship against a prolonged series of attacks.

Upgrades to the Phalanx have occurred on a regular basis since its introduction, including enhancements to the radar system and the addition of other types of tracking sensors such as Forward-Looking Infrared (FLIR) camera's. These updates provide the Phalanx an ever improving ability to accurately track an incoming threat and precisely define its position. The most modern version of the Phalanx, introduced in 2015, is able to defeat the latest generation of fast moving anti-shipping cruise missiles, automatically adjusting the targeting trajectory to compensate for any last moment evasive maneuvers that the missiles may make. The system can also engage approaching small manned and unmanned watercraft which could potentially be laden with explosives.

As the American's were developing the Phalanx, the Soviets were concurrently working on their own version of a CIWS, the A-213-Vympel-A. Unlike Western nations the Russians decided not to integrate their tracking system directly into the weapon station but rather to maintain it as a separate unit. This approach was chosen by the Russians to permit placing many weapon stations on their ships at a lower per unit cost. The weapon station associated with a

Vympel-A tracking system is the AK-630, a six-barreled 30 mm autocannon. Using a single tracking system to control multiple AK-630 units may save cost, but it has the disadvantage of slowing down the systems overall response time. Targeting by the Vympel-A for the AK-630's is provided by a combination of radar and electro-optical trackers together with a laser range finder. The Russians claim that the Vympel-A can detect targets out to a 4 miles (7 km) radius and engage aerial targets as far away as 2.5 miles (4 km). The large powerful radar of the Vympel-A emits a stronger beam than CIWS fielded by Western nations, making the Vympel-A difficult to jam electronically.

It is interesting to note that the Russian Cruiser Moskva was equipped with a Vympel-A CIWS and six AK-630 units. Despite the heavy compliment of gun stations, this system proved itself completely inadequate at defending the ship from the approaching pair of relatively simple Neptune anti-shipping cruise missiles. It is unknown if the radar system failed to detect the incoming missiles, if it responded too slowly in firing the AK-630's, if the AK-630's fired but missed the targets, or if the system was inoperable at the time of the attack. Regardless, this event does not speak well for the performance of the Vympel-A CIWS.

A pair of AK-630's of the Vympel-A CIWS equipped on-board the Cruiser Moskva before it was sunk.
Credit: sputniknews.com

Other CIWS systems later developed by the Russian's include the Kashtan, the Palma and the Pantsir-M. The most recent is the Pantsir-M, which was introduced in 2018. It combines both a rotary cannon and short-range defensive missiles into one unit. The addition of missiles to supplement the autocannon offers a chance to engage targets at a greater range than with only the gun. Firing its missiles first, the auto-cannon of the Pantsir-M then provides a reserve point defense for any missed threats. The system can track and engage up to four targets simultaneously and each Pantsir-M tracking unit can co-ordinate a response from up to three individual weapon stations. The Pantsir-M is inherently jam resistant is equipped with an Identify Friend vs Foe (IFF) system to avoid the possibility of a fratricide event.

The missile used by the Pantsir-M is known as the 9M337 by the Russians and designated at SA-24's by NATO. It is a two-stage missile with a range of 6 miles (10 km) and able to attain Mach 4 in flight. The missile is guided toward its intended target by both radar and a beam rider laser. SA-24's are said to be able to make course corrections while in flight to adjust for any defensive maneuvers taken by the incoming threat. Missiles for the Pantsir-M are auto-loaded, with less than one minute between when one is launched and the next is ready. Other sources suggest that the Hermes-K air-defense missile may also be used with the system. The Pantsir-M has only recently completed field trials and is yet to be installed in a service condition on any Russian naval vessels. A version of the Pantsir-M is also available for sale on the international arms market.

The imposing looking Pantsir-M
Credit: defenceturk.net

A Chinese Type 730 CIWS in action.
Credit: globaltimes.cn

China in turn developed their seven barreled 30 mm Type 730 CIWS. The system is stated to be effective to a range of 2 miles (3 km) against air threats and 3 miles (5km) against seaborn threats. Incoming threats are tracked by a radar unit in a set-up similar to that used with the Phalanx. The radar is sensitive enough to identify incoming threats out to a distance of 5 miles (8 km). The radar data is supplemented by an electro-optical system, a laser rangefinder and IR cameras. Data from each of these sensors is collated to define a precise firing solution for the aiming of the gun. Armor Piercing Discarded Sabot (APDS) rounds are employed against air targets at a range less than 2.5 km, while High-Explosive (HE) rounds are used for air targets out to 3.5 km and surface targets to 5 km. Newer versions of the Type 730 also include the addition of short-range missiles to provide a layered defense.

There are also CIWS systems produced by various European nations. All CIWS are similar in many regards to one another, but each also possesses some unique characteristics. The chart below shows the performance specifications of a typical American, European, Russian and Chinese CIWS, providing for a quick comparison reference source between them.

	Type 730	**Kashtan**	**Phalanx**	**Millennium**
Developed by	China	Russia	USA	Switzerland
Weight	9,800 kg (21,600 lb)	15,500 kg (34,200 lb)	6,200 kg (13,700 lb)	3,300 kg (7,300 lb)
Armament	30 mm (1.2 in) 7 barreled Gatling Gun	30 mm (1.2 in) 6 barreled GSh-6-30 Gatling Gun	20 mm (0.79 in) 6 barreled M61 Vulcan Gatling Gun	35 mm (1.4 in) single barreled Oerlikon Millennium 35 mm Naval Gun
Rate of fire	7,000 rounds/min	5,000 rounds/min	4,500 rounds/min	1000 rounds/min
Effective Range	3,000 m (9,800 ft)	5,000 m (16,400 ft)	2,000 m (6,600 ft)	3,500 m (11,500 ft)
Ammunition storage	500 rounds	2,000 rounds	1,550 rounds	252 rounds
Muzzle velocity	1,100 m (3,600 ft/s)	1,100 m (3,600 ft/s)	1,100 m (3,600 ft/s)	1,175 m (3,855 ft/s)
Elevation	−25 to +85 degrees	−25 to +85 degrees	−25 to +85 degrees	−15 to +85 degrees
Speed in elevation	100 degrees per second	50 degrees per second	115 degrees per second	70 degrees per second
Traverse	360 °	360 °	360 °	360 °
Speed in Traverse	100 degrees per second	70 degrees per second	115 degrees per second	120 degrees per second
In service	2007	1989	1980	2003

Anti-Missile Missiles

While gatling gun styled anti-missile technologies were effective, they could only engage incoming missiles at mere seconds before impact with the ship. Therefore navies sought to supplement these with anti-missile missiles to provide a layered defense which would provide them more than one shot at the cat, so to speak. Early versions of these short-range anti-missile missiles were developed from existing anti-aircraft missiles. While some nations like China and Russia incorporated these directly into the gatling gun radar system, Western nations have generally chosen to add such missile systems as stand-alone solutions with their own optimized radar units. These missiles have also grown in size over the years so that they are able to engage targets at ever increasing distances. While initially developed to protect ships, both gun-based CIWS and anti-missile missiles have been modified for land use to also provide protection to airbases, barracks and key command and communication structures.

The evolution of missiles from the anti-aircraft role to the anti-missile role was a gradual one, requiring incremental improvements of their guidance and maneuvering capabilities. The first missile defense missiles were designed to intercept anti-shipping cruise missiles. This was a natural evolution, as early cruise missiles were often about the same size of a small jet aircraft, and flew at about the same speed and altitude as one. In response cruise missile technologies also improved to make the missiles more challenging to intercept. Techniques included introducing stealth features and jamming systems to the cruise missiles, increasing their speed and providing them the ability to take evasive maneuvers as they approached their target. Anti-shipping cruise missiles also began to fly ever closer to the surface of the water, making them more challenging for radar to detect and specifically to track. Anti-missile radar and missile systems in turn had to improve to become better at picking up the fainter RCS of cruise missiles, overcoming jamming, tracking faster incoming cruise missiles, making adjustments to account for missiles making evasive maneuvers, and to be able to differentiate incoming sea-skimming cruise missiles from the close background reflections of the moving water surface. Improvement in the one technology continually necessitated improvement in the other, a common factor constantly driving innovative weapons development.

A significant issue in countering sea-skimming missiles is not only that they are difficult to differentiate from the surface over which they are skimming, but also the limited detection range a missile-defense system has to identify the incoming threat. Recall that surface radar only has a detection range of 20 miles (32 km) against surface targets, as limited by the curvature of the Earth. A missile incoming at 500 mph will close that distance in less than 2.5 minutes. This is why CIWS are designed to destroy incoming threats close to the ship – any missile they can detect will always be close to the ship. Intercepting incoming sea-skimming cruise missiles with missiles at ranges greater than 20 miles requires aircraft-based radar to pick up on the incoming missile threat and for the radar to be able to quickly transmit intercept co-ordinates to the shipped based anti-missile missile system. This is no small feat, requiring powerful airborne radar and a highly integrated communication and command structure.

In time improvements in the sophistication of guidance systems permitted naval based anti-missile missiles to track and engage ever smaller threats at ever greater ranges that were travelling at ever faster speeds. These anti-missile missiles are able to engage a range of incoming missile threats, including both sea skimming cruise missiles and high-altitude ballistic missiles. Many of the resulting missiles are capable of defending both the ship from which it is launched as well as other allied ships, as was the case with the Gloucester protecting the Missouri. Land based anti-missile missiles were also developed in parallel with their naval cousins, evolving as well from existing anti-aircraft missiles. These in turn developed to the point that they were equally able to engage incoming land-attack cruise missiles and high-altitude ballistic missiles. The US initiated development of very capable anti-missile missiles and remains by far the leader in regards to this technology. The Russians and Chinese however are attempting to catch up, and the Chinese in particular are investing heavily in the development of missile defense systems.

US Missile Defense

Initial American anti-missile missile development sought to complement the gatling guns of the Phalanx CIWS with a missile system. The result was the RIM-116 Rolling Airframe Missile (RAM). The name of the missile is derived from the introduction of a rolling motion that stabilizes the missiles flight path. The RAM was developed from the USAF Sidewinder missile. In service since 1992, the small short-range RAM cost $900,000 USD a piece. They are used by the USN as well as the navies of Germany, Japan, Greece, Turkey, South Korea, Saudi Arabia, Egypt and Mexico. RAM's are 9 feet (2.8 meters) long, weigh 162 pounds (74 kg) and are propelled by a solid fuel rocket motor. Quickly accelerating to reach a velocity of greater than Mach 2, RAMS can strike at targets out to a distance of 6 miles (10 km) and are equipped with a 24 pound (11 kg) blast fragmentation warhead.

There are two launcher systems available for the RAM. The SeaRAM system hold 11 RAM's and is integrated with the Phalanx. During launch the RAM's are guided toward their targets by passive radio frequency in which the linked Phalanx radar and electro-optical system provides the missile with attack co-ordinates. Alternatively an independent launcher containing 21 RAM's is networked to acquire target identification and tracking information through the ships radar and other sensors. With either launch system the RAM's can be fired individually or in waves. Once launched the RAM uses its own infrared homing and radio frequency tracking sensors to precisely home in on the assigned target. Radio frequency tracking involves homing in on any radio waves being emitted by the incoming missile as it relays positional data back to its own launch site. A four-axis independent control actuator system adjusts the missile flight surfaces to keep its direction oriented toward the target, countering any maneuvers the incoming threat may make in an effort to avoid interception by the RAM. It is claimed that the RAM has a successful engagement accuracy of 95%.

A SeaRAM launcher for RIM-116 Rolling Airframe missiles integrated with the radar of the Phalanx.
Credit: whitefleet.net

The RIM-162 Evolved SeaSparrow Missile (ESSM) was then developed as a medium range missile defense missile. The ESSM was developed from the earlier RIM-7 anti-aircraft Sea Sparrow missile, itself developed from the Sparrow air-to-air missile. The enhancements provided to the ESSM make it capable of not only engaging incoming missile threats, but it is able to counter supersonic anti-ship missiles that are capable of performing evasive maneuvers. The ESSM is able to rapidly adjust its course to compensate for an incoming missiles effort to evade it through use of integrated strakes and skid-to-turn aerodynamics. Being small and slender, four of these missiles can be carried together in a VLS tube. The ESSM is 620 pound (280 kg), 12 foot long (3.66 meters) and reaches a peak velocity of Mach 4. Guided toward its assigned target by semi-active radar with a mid-course correction datalink, the missile engages its own radar for the terminal approach. A proximity fuse detonates its 86 pound (39 kg) blast fragmentation warhead upon closest approach to the target.

RIM-162 Evolved SeaSparrow Missile following launch
Credit: airforce-technology.com

In service since 2004 and produced at a unit cost of $1.8 million USD, the missile is used by a broad collection of nations including the US, Australia, Canada, Germany, Japan, the Netherlands, Norway, Finland, Denmark, Greece, Mexico, Thailand and Turkey. The missile has a maximum effective range of out to 30 miles (50 km). The ESSM is intended to be used as the mid-range missile interceptor as part of a naval fleets layered missile defense shield. When the fleet is attacked by successive waves of anti-shipping missiles, as is the anticipated tactic of an opponent, the ESSM can be fired in massed salvos. It constitutes the mid-layer of the shield, engaging missiles that penetrate the first line of longer-range defensive missiles and similarly serving to protect all ships of the fleet. The RAM and Phalanx then remain as the inner defense and the last-line-of-defense systems for each specific ship.

The long range missile interceptors for the USN are the SM-2 and the SM-6. The RIM-66 Standard, or SM-2, was first introduced in 1967 as an anti-aircraft missile and has received innumerable upgrades since this time. The Mach 3.5 missile is powered by a dual-thrust solid fuel rocket and has a range of out to 100 miles (160 km). Destroying its target with a blast fragmentation warhead and with latest version guided to the target by semi-active radar, the missile has proven itself effective in destroying incoming missile threats. In 2016 the Arleigh-Burke destroyer USS Mason had an attack launched upon it by Yemenis rebels in which five anti-shipping missiles were simultaneously launched at the vessel. SM-2's were fired in salvo and successfully destroyed the targets and defended the ship. The RIM-174 SM-6 began to be produced in 2009, uses a two stage solid fuel rocket to propel it to Mach 3.5, has an effective range of 150 miles (240 km) and destroys its target with a 140 pound (63 kg) blast fragmentation warhead. Guided to its target by semi-active and active radar, the SM-6 is able to engage high flying aircraft, incoming cruise missiles and can even engage and destroy incoming ballistic missiles during the terminal stage of their descent.

A SM-6 during launch from a VLS on the USS John Paul Jones
Credit: Wikipedia.org

The American army has also developed missile systems capable of destroying incoming missile threats targeting land-based positions. Similar to the navies approach, the army sought to improve the performance of existing anti-aircraft missiles to the point that they could engage incoming ballistic missile threats. This effort began with the ubiquitous MIM-104 Patriot, a long-range surface-to-air missile (SAM) system first introduced in 1984. The name Patriot is an acronym for 'Phased Array Tracking Radar to Intercept on Target'. The US has already built tens of thousands of these missiles. The Patriot is a prolific missile system with a wide distribution of usage. Currently the Patriot missile is used by the US, the Netherlands, Poland, Germany, Egypt, Japan, Israel, Saudi Arabia, Kuwait, Taiwan, Greece, Spain, UAE, Quartar, Romania, South Korea and Jordan. The missile has been used during both the Persian Gulf War and the Iraq War, as well as during Israeli-Gaza conflicts and Saudi Arabian conflicts to defend these nations from cross-border attacks.

The first prolific use of Patriot missile batteries occurred during the Persian Gulf War in 1991. As the Iraqi air force was destroyed largely on the ground by US combat aircraft, Patriots had little opportunity to be engaged in the anti-aircraft role. As a consequence US forces attempted to use their Patriot's to intercept the Scud missiles fired by Iraq toward Israel and Saudi Arabia. The missiles proved themselves to be reasonably capable in this role and therefore a significant investment was made to enhance the missiles anti-missile capabilities. During the Iraq War of 2003, the anti-ballistic missile capabilities of the enhanced Patriot batteries were successfully demonstrated. Since this time most nations currently using the Patriot missile system employ it principally in the anti-ballistic missile (ABM) role. The Patriot was in fact the first missile created that was able to successful able to engage and destroy incoming ballistic missiles.

Each Patriot missile is 19 feet (5.8 meter) long, weighs 1500 pounds (700 kg) and is armed with a 200 pound (90 kg) high explosive blast fragmentation warhead detonated by a proximity fuse. Patriots are truck and trailer towed and mounted and an entire missile battery can be set up inside of an hour. Multiple Patriot missiles are pre-loaded into each battery and these can be quickly reloaded once launched. A Patriot battery consists of a number of inter-functional systems that provide the system the ability to identify, track and engage incoming targets without human input. These include a radar detection and tracking system, a fire control system, a communications, command and control system and a missile guidance system. The missiles can engage aircraft out to 100 miles (160 km) distance and ballistic missiles out to 22 miles (35 km), at a maximum ceiling height of 15 miles (24 km). The missiles reach a maximum velocity of Mach 4.1. During its flight time midcourse corrections are provided via feedback between the ground-based tracking radar and servo actuating steering fins to keep the missile on target while a terminal guidance system engages as the target is approached.

Launching of a Patriot missile
Credit: businessinsider.com

Russian Missile Defense

The Russians have also developed their own sophisticated and capable anti-aircraft and anti-missile missile defense system. The S-400 Triumf, referred to by NATO as the SA-21 Growler, was introduced in 2007 as an evolution of its predecessor, the S-300. Both systems make use of a number of different sized missiles that are stored together within the truck mounted launch canisters. Larger sized missiles have greater range but also cost more than the smaller missiles. This allows a single S-400 launch system to provide long-range, medium-range and close-range anti-aircraft / anti-missile defense to a large region surrounding each missile battery. Each battery has its own tracking and interception radar along with its own command, control and communication system together with its core of processing computers. This equipment is contained within and transported on an associated trailer. The systems radar are high powered units which are thereby inherently resilient against jamming efforts.

Each S-400 missile battalion consists of 9 launchers, 120 missiles, and command and support vehicles. The entire system comes at a cost of approximately $300 million USD. Once an S-400 missile battalion is set up it provides air interception capabilities over a radius of many hundreds of miles through a series of four missile types. The 40N6E can intercept incoming threats out to a range of 250 miles (400 km). The 48N6 provides interception capabilities to 155 miles (250 km). While the 9M96E2 and the 9M96E have effective ranges of 75 miles (120 km) and 25 miles (40 km) respectively. Each launch canister can hold four of the smaller sized missiles and two of the larger sized missiles. All missiles rely on explosive warheads to destroy their intended targets. The missile with the longest range, as well as the two with shorter ranges, are equipped with their own active homing radar for the terminal approach upon their target, while the middle range missiles engage targets solely upon signals transmitted from the system targeting radar unit.

S-400 Triumf transport truck and missile storage canisters on the move
Credit: defenceview.in

The Russians claim that the S-400 radar system can detect incoming ballistic missiles to a range of 145 miles (230 km), non-stealth fighter aircraft to a range of 245 miles (390 km) and non-stealth strategic bombers to a range of 350 miles (570 km). The system is stated to be able to engage incoming missile threats moving at up to Mach 14 and it is claimed to be able to track up to 80 threats simultaneously. While some of this might be exaggeration or very best case situations, the S-400 remains regarded as an excellent anti-aircraft, anti-missile system. The S-300, upon which the S-400 is based upon, has proven itself very effective during the Russian invasion of Ukraine. Operated by the Ukrainians, their older S-300 systems have been used to good effect in depriving the Russians of their goal in achieving air superiority, thwarting Russian plans to dominate the local airspace. It is noteworthy that these older S-300 systems are able to shoot down the most modern Soviet aircraft, including their MiG-29 and Su-35. This speaks volumes about both the quality of their anti-aircraft systems and perhaps equally the lack of quality in their aircraft and piloting skills.

A group of S-400's launchers in their operations position. Note the vertical position of the launch tubes. Missiles are initially directed upward and therefore provide 360 coverage. The radar command vehicle can be seen in the background.
Credit: sputniknews.com

The Russians have also claimed that their panoramic radar is sensitive enough to be able to receive radar reflections off of stealth aircraft that approach the radar with 93 miles (150 km). Of course this is based on a given RCS for an aircraft, which current stealth aircraft may have lower values than, or may only produce at certain angles while executing high turns or while their weapons bay doors are open. Truth is that Russia would have very little data to judge their ability to detect the stealth aircraft of other nations upon. They are more likely making projections based on detection of their own stealth aircraft which have higher RCS's than US equivalents, particularly at angles other than that of a direct approach. It is thought by American military specialists that the S-400 can probably actually detect an F-35 at about 25 miles (40 km) distance with the various high performance radar systems it has at its disposal. Remember that 'stealth' implies difficult to detect, not impossible to detect. Therefore stealth aircraft can approach an opponents radar unit much more closely than a conventional aircraft, but ultimately it will still be detected. This however gives a stealth aircraft a great advantage, as it can launch its own long-range weapons at a radar facility beyond the range at which that radar can detect the approaching aircraft. Equipped with missiles with a range greater than 25 miles, a F-35 can detect and destroy a S-400 launch site before that launch site even detects the presence of the F-35. That is the true power of stealth.

The Russians have made the S-400, as well as their S-300, available for international sale. To date China has purchased S-400's, while Saudi Arabia, Turkey, India and Belarus have expressed interest in procuring the system. This has become a point of contention with the US for those countries also interested in purchasing the F-35, as the American military does not want anyone studying how to best use the S-400 to counter their most modern and sophisticated aircraft. A great deal about how to effectively detect an aircraft can be achieved by practice and pairing the S-400 with the F-35 could potentially expose vulnerabilities in both systems. Studies by a radar system against a stealth aircraft can be used to determine which angles the aircraft has a higher radar cross-section (RCS) along. Strategic placement of the radar units can then exploit these known vulnerabilities by positioned them such that they issue radar waves at directions toward the aircraft with the known higher RCS, thus increasing the probability of detecting and specifically successfully tracking them.

Israeli Missile Defense

Other nations of course have also invested heavily in missile defense systems. Key among these is Israel. As well as preparing for a peer-on-peer conflict, Israel also focuses its missile development programs on countering opponents who not infrequently lob large volleys of munitions across the Israel border toward their population centers. Therefore the first layer of their missile defense shield is capable of destroying incoming small ballistic rockets, mortar rounds and artillery shells, as these are the threats which they most commonly face. They also have anti-missile missiles able to engage cruise missiles and ballistic missiles, as such threats could come from various neighbours. Successful outcomes from this effort include the development of Iron Dome, the Arrow and David's Sling. These three missile systems together provide a layered defense for the borders of Israel, with the larger missiles taking on more challenging targets while the shorter-range missiles engage simpler threats.

Iron Dome missile defense battery in northern Israel
Credit: Getty Images

Iron Dome is designed to engage low altitude threats at short range. In service since 2011 the system has seen significant engagements to date. The lowest costing system of the three tiers, an Iron Dome missile battery costs $50 million USD. Each battery consists of 3 or 4 launchers and each of these carries 20 interceptors. Therefore the cost per interception is only about $100,000, a low price to pay to destroy incoming threats but expensive compared to an artillery or mortar round. Each Iron Dome missile is 9.8 foot (3 meter) long, has a 6.3 inch (160 mm) diameter and weighs 200 pounds (90 kg). The single stage rocket motor quickly propels the missile to a speed of Mach 2.2. The system is operable under all weather conditions and is effective to a distance of 43 miles (70 km). It is able to engage small free-falling munitions such as mortar rounds and artillery shells as well as short-range rockets and UAV's.

Detection and targeting information for the Iron Dome is provided by a radar system and relayed to the individual missiles through a battle management and weapon control system. Following launch the missile guides itself toward the target through on-board electro-optical sensors and adjusts its course using steering fins. The warhead of the highly maneuverable missile then explodes upon closest approach to the target via a proximity fuze. The battle management system calculates if the trajectory of the incoming threat will land in a populated area and only engages them when this is a possibility. This permits the system to conserve missiles and prioritize their use on significant threats. Iron Dome is capable of engaging multiple incoming targets simultaneously. In theatre the system has so far successfully intercepted thousands of incoming threats. In 2021 alone over 4300 rockets were fired by Hamas from Gaza into Israel over a 10 day period. Hamas attempted to overwhelm Israel defenses through lobbing massed barrages of munitions launched simultaneously. Iron Dome intercepted and destroyed 90% of those incoming threats assessed as heading toward populated regions, demonstrating its ability to counter saturation rocket attack tactics. Hamas also attempted to attack Israel by deploying drones which were loaded with explosives. These too were engaged and neutralized.

David's Sling is a medium range anti-ballistic surface-to-air missile (SAM) developed by Israel with technical and financial support from the US. Entering service in 2017, David's sling is a two-stage missile with a range of 186 miles (300 km). The missile associated with David's sling is known as the Stunner. Following target designation and lock-on by a ground-based radar unit, a launched Stunner is guided toward the target by both an on-board AESA millimeter 3D radar and a dual electro-optical and infrared imaging seeker. The arrangement of these sensors provides for an asymmetric 360-degree capability. A 3-way data link to ground based command and control centers also allows for target re-designation during the missiles flight time. The warhead is a hit-to-kill kinetic energy vehicle. The system was designed to intercept medium range rockets but can also engage enemy aircraft, UAV's, cruise missiles.

Launching of a Stunner missile from a David's Sling missile battery
Credit: defencetalk.com

Israel has also worked in partnership with India to produce the Barkak 8 long-range surface-to-air missile. Israeli provided design authority for the missile while India is engaged in the construction of the missiles. Entering service in 2016 the missile system is currently employed with the Indian Army, Navy and Airforce. The missile is also used by the Israeli Army and was sold to the Azerbaijan Air Force. The missile is 180 inches in length (4.5 meters), weighs 606 pounds (275 kg), is powered by a two-stage pulsed rocket motor and wields a 132 pound (60 kg) warhead detonated by a proximity fuse. The missile has an operational range of 93 miles (150 km) and a flight ceiling of 19 miles (30 km). During flight the missile attains Mach 3 and is guided to its target through both a RF/IIR seeker and a two-way data link. The missile is able to engage aircraft, helicopters, UAV's and cruise missiles.

An Arrow-3 long-range missile battery on display
Credit: jns.org

Missile Defense of Other Nations

The Chinese have also developed a number of air defense weapon systems. The HQ-22 is a medium range anti-aircraft /anti-missile system that entered service is 2017 and is used by both China and Serbia. The missile is 23 feet (7 meters) long, weights 2870 pounds (1300 kg) and has a 400 pound (180 kg) warhead that is detonated through a proximity fuse. The missile has a range of 105 miles (170 km) and an altitude ceiling of 17 miles (27 km). Guidance is through semi-active radar homing and radio-command. Semi-active homing is the default guidance system, while radio-command is engaged when strong electronic interference is encountered. A HQ-22 missile battery is fully mobile and consists of three launcher vehicles each armed with four missiles, a radar vehicle and a command and coordination vehicle.

An HQ-22 air denial missile battery, showing radar equipped vehicle in the middle.
Credit: military-today.com

The HQ-22 is one of the principal air defense weapons of China, being built and deployed in large numbers. It is claimed to be effective in engaging aircraft, helicopters, UAV's, ballistic missiles and cruise missiles. It is claimed that a HQ-22 missile battery can engage up to six air targets at once, firing missiles at each target in pairs. Launching two missiles at a target is actually standard practice for also Russian and Western systems as well. It is much more challenging for an aircraft or missile to take effective evasive maneuvers against two co-ordinated incoming missiles. It is thought that the HQ-22 system also incorporates advanced electronic warfare countermeasures (ECM) and that it might be even more effective in detecting stealth targets than the S-400.

Western European nations often purchase American air defense systems, but they have also developed a number of modern and effective domestic systems as well. Aster is a family of missiles co-developed by Italy and France. The Aster 15 is the short and medium range air denial weapon, which has a range of up to 19 miles (30 km). The Aster 30 is the long-range missile with a range of 75 miles (120 km). Both missiles entered service in 2001. Each is propelled by a solid propellant two-stage rocket and is equipped with a 33 pound (15 kg) fragmentation warhead triggered by a proximity fuse. The Aster 15 attains a maximum flight speed of Mach 3.5 and the Aster 30 attains Mach 4.5. Guidance is provided through an inertial guidance system with an up-link during the initial flight stage and through an active RF seeker for the terminal approach upon the target. The vertically launched canister stored missiles can be land or sea based and are effective in engaging high-performance aircraft, missiles and supersonic sea-skimming anti-ship cruise missiles. The Aster family of missiles are available upon the internationally arms market and are used by many other countries besides France and Italy. The UK has purchased the missiles, referring to them as Sea Vipers.

An Aster missile following launch
Credit: i-hls.com

Directed Energy Weapons

While the use of missiles to shoot down other missiles is a relatively new development, an even more recent development is the use of directed energy weapons to either destroy incoming missile threats or to disorient their guidance systems. Directed energy weapons used in missile defense include lasers, electro-magnetic pulse (EMP) and radio frequency (RF) directed energy sources. Lasers have been used on the battlefield since the 1970's, soon after their invention. They have long been used in laser rangefinders and laser designators. During the Vietnam war they were used as laser designators to direct Paveway smart bombs onto targets such as bridges that were otherwise challenging to hit precisely.

As laser technology matured and their intensity increased, they have also proven themselves effective in the missile defense role. Medium intensity lasers are directed toward incoming missiles that rely upon infrared guidance. The concentrated heat source of the laser blinds the missiles infrared detection sensor, in a manner similar to shining a bright light into someone's eyes. Some nations such as China have employed lasers in this precise role - directing them toward aircraft to make it difficult for the pilot to see their surroundings. High intensity lasers can be used to destroy incoming missiles by burning a hole through the missile body and damaging equipment within it. This approach can be used to destroy both guided missiles as well as unguided munitions, such as unguided rockets, mortar shells and even artillery shells. They have also been used to good effect in destroying UAV's.

The power of a laser is a function of the electrical power available. The greater the power unit output, the more intense a laser may be. Thus the US Navy, with the large size of their ships, their powerful engines and the associated ability to generate and store huge amounts of electrical energy, have led the way in the development and deployment of battlefield lasers. The USN have also begun to investigate the use of medium powered lasers on aircraft in the role of dazzlers. The SHIELD (Self-

Protect High-Energy Laser Demonstrator) has been installed on carrier-based jet fighters to test its ability to effectively blind incoming infrared homing missiles.

The first air denial laser weapon system operationally deployed was the AN/SEQ-3 LaWS (Laser Weapon System). This system was installed on board the USS Ponce, a floating naval base ship, in 2014. These ships are both large and difficult to maneuver, while also not heavily armed for either attack or defense. Therefore they are vulnerable to attack and rely upon escort missile destroyers to protect them. It is expected that opponents will use UAV's in the role of collecting and providing targeting co-ordinates for anti-shipping missile systems, and that vessels such as naval base ships will be priority objectives. With its 30 kW power rating the LaWS is therefore designed to disable or destroy UAV's that approach US naval craft. For small and medium UAV's, LaWS burns through the body of the UAV to destroy it. For larger UAV's the laser is used to blind the UAV's electro-optical sensors.

A LaWS, In firing position outside of its protective shelter.
Credit: 1boon.kakao.com

Two other systems developed by the USN are ODIN (Optical Dazzling Interdictor, Navy) and HELIOS (High-Energy Laser and Integrated Optical-Dazzler with Surveillance). ODIN is intended to blind the sensors of approaching UAV's, functioning as a form of 'dazzler', though more focused and with a longer range than traditional IR based dazzlers. ODIN has already been installed on-board an Arleigh Burke-class guided missile destroyer for sea trials. HELIOS is a larger laser system in the 150 kW range. While in the proto-type development stage, it is designed to independently identify, track and destroy incoming threats. The intent it to synchronize HELIOS together with a ships existing CIWS to provide a more comprehensive last line of defense response.

Currently the USN is also developing 300 kW lasers. Lasers of this power would be capable of destroying cruise missiles and closely approaching aircraft. Proximity is key as the atmosphere distorts the light within a laser beam, so the power delivered upon a target is reduced with range. Atmospheric conditions also have a significant effect upon laser intensity with range. Air heavily saturated with water moisture such as foggy conditions or clouds quickly degrades the laser intensity. Therefore lasers are best suited for engaging incoming threats as a last line of defense. Interestingly, there are plans to integrate a 300 to 500 kW laser system into Virginia-class submarines. Power to the laser would be provide by the massive 30 MW output of the subs nuclear reactor. Though still in development, such a laser could rapidly dispatch incoming missile attacks or strike aircraft approaching the sub while it is surfaced and vulnerable.

Laser based weapons have also been installed on aircraft as an offensive weapon. The USAF has powerful lasers installed on large aircraft capable of destroying ICBM's during their launch phase. The AC-130J Ghostrider is a Special Forces aircraft based on the Hercules chassis that mounts a radar guided 105 mm howitzer, 30 mm autocannon, launches AGM-176 Griffin missiles and drops 250 pound GPS guided bombs. It is now also going to mount an offensive laser system intended to shoot down UAV's and cause damage to ground targets. The laser can be used to damage radar equipment, rockets launch sites and ammunition/fuel depots. In this ground attack role the laser is behaving essentially as a long-range blow torch, blowing holes through structures to damage equipment or detonate ammo and fuel.

Mobile land-based laser systems with portable towed electrical powerplants have also been developed and are being deployed. ATHENA (Advanced Test High Energy Asset) was developed for the USAF to provide a defensive system for air bases. It is capable of simultaneously engaging and destroying multiple incoming UAV's. While both the US Army and US Marine Corps have installed lasers directly onto wheeled vehicles to counter incoming threats. In 2022 the US Army began to employ 50 kW laser systems mounted on Stryker combat vehicles. Known as DE M-SHORAD (Directed Energy Maneuver-Short Range Air Defense), the system is able to engage low flying aircraft, UAV's, rockets, mortar shells and artillery rounds. While the USMC employs the Compact Laser Weapon System (CLaWS) mounted upon their Joint Light Tactical Vehicles (JLTV) to neutralize UAV's.

Israel has designed and fielded the Ion Beam laser defense system. Meant to work together with Arrow 3, David's Sling and Iron Dome, it is also referred to as Light Blade. Entering service in 2020, funding for its development was largely provided by the US. An Iron Beam battery consists of an air defense radar, a command and control unit and two High Energy Laser (HEL) systems. The system utilizes directed energy laser beams to engage incoming small threats such as UAV's, short range rockets, artillery shells and mortar bombs. Data from a targeting radar is fed to the laser system, which then orients the lasers at the target. The dual fiber-optic lasers are discharged together and destroy incoming threats by applying the lasers to the target for a period of 4 to 5 seconds. During this time the lasers burns through the target, causing it to detonate or otherwise be destroyed. The system provides a low cost per shot engagement system. With a range of 4.3 miles (7 km), it is effective as neutralizing threats that penetrate the other defensive shields or are too small to justify using an expensive missile to counter. Overall the system has a lower operational cost than missile based systems, requires less manpower to operate and in theory can engage an unlimited number of targets, not limited by ordnance restrictions. By comparison, where a missile launch costs approximately $100k a shot, firing the laser costs about $2000 a shot.

Another method to use Directed Energy as an air denial system is to direct intense radio frequency waves at either radar or communication systems to interfere with their operation. This technique results in a large undiscernible background white noise, which blankets and obscures the more subtle intended signal. Radar systems on some modern US and European aircraft for example can be focused and directed at an incoming radar homing missile to blind it, similar to the method of using lasers to blind heat seeking missiles. Radio energy directed at a missile can also interfere with the communication link between its air, sea or ground-based control system. Another approach is to direct an intense microwave frequency beam at a missile to fry its on-board computer circuitry by creating a localized Electro-Magnetic Pulse (EMP). The EMP energy acts to ionize the air surrounding the target, causing unprotected electrical components to be short circuited. This can temporarily disable those circuits or destroy them entirely. This method is suitable for crippling UAV's and both hand portable units and vehicle mounted systems have been developed and deployed by various militaries around the world.

Russian Tor-M2U EMP cannon, on an exercise in February 2019.
Credit: Konstantin Morozov, Russian Ministry of Defense

UNMANNED AERIAL VEHICLES

The use of unmanned systems has been growing exponentially over the last 20 years. Seeing their first large scale employment during the Iraq and Afghanistan Wars in a surveillance role, their use became ubiquitous during the Russian invasion of Ukraine in which they served both as surveillance platforms and loitering munitions. While Unmanned Aerial Vehicles (UAV's) are the most familiar type of unmanned vehicle to many of us, unmanned systems also include Unmanned Ground Vehicles (UGV), Unmanned Naval Vehicles (UNV) and Unmanned Submersible Vehicles (USV). The idea of using remotely or autonomously operated unmanned systems for air, ground and sea operations is not a new one. The Germans in WWII used a remotely controlled small tracked vehicle with an embedded anti-tank mine. Old aircraft have also long been converted to being remotely operated and then used as aerial test targets. It is these modified aircraft for which the term 'drone' was first used and eventually became synonymous with UAV's.

The development of UAV's and cruise missiles occurred together, as a winged UAV is essentially a remotely controlled cruise missile, while a cruise missile is an autonomously operating UAV. The intended role for each is different though, with UAV's initially serving as surveillance platforms and cruise missiles functioning as flying bombs. These lines of course are being blurred as the technologies and roles of both UAVs and cruise missile progress and merge. The latest cruise missiles can be selected to loiter over a target area and survey the ground below to seek out suitable targets. While modern UAV's incorporate various levels of autonomous features. They are also being designed as Unmanned Combat Aerial Vehicles (UCAV) which are able to launch attacks against targets with munitions, and as Loitering Munitions (so-called suicide or kamikaze drones), in which the UAV is the munition, propelling itself toward identified yet unsuspecting targets.

The US first began developing and deploying dedicated surveillance UAV's during the Vietnam War. Many of the piloted aircraft used in this role were large and noisy and therefore easily spotted from the ground, making them vulnerable to anti-aircraft systems. Aircraft equipped with powerful engines can also only remain over the target area for a limited time, consuming their fuel far too quickly to have a prolonged loitering duration. Dedicated reconnaissance UAV's are constructed with broad wings to provide high lift and small engines to reduce fuel consumption. So where an aircraft used in the surveillance role might be limited to performing a half hour or so of reconnaissance, a light UAV can loiter for the better part of the day over the target area. UAV's are also inexpensive compared to a jet aircraft, as well as present very small and quiet targets. Therefore they are challenging for an opponent to detect, and if they are detected, difficult to acquire a lock-on to. Being unmanned and inexpensive, UAV's are often considered expendable assets, with the loss of a UAV to ground fire bringing no significant grief to family members or military budgets.

Examples of early UAV's. They were often comparatively small and launched from mobile rail systems. For recovery they typically deployed parachutes.
Credit: th.bing.com (left image) & airaffairs.com.au (right image)

These early UAV's saw only limited service. Their operational range was limited, as were their capabilities. The development of advanced remotely piloted surveillance UAV's began in earnest in the 1990's by the US. Their accelerated development at this point of time was a result of the advent of high-speed computers. The introduction of sophisticated CPU's and eventually embedded AI functions into the UAV's meant that their capabilities were enhanced to the point that they exceeded those of piloted aircraft in many regards. These dedicated surveillance UAV's were quickly expanded in their roles to include attack capabilities. This trend parallels the development of early aircraft. In WWI aircraft were first used simply for surveillance, providing a bird's eye view of the opponents trench lines and artillery positions. Guns were soon added so that the aircraft could shoot down an opponent's recon aircraft, while bombs able to be dropped on an enemy position were a later addition. Manned aircraft after WWI soon became specialized as reconnaissance aircraft, ground attack aircraft, aerial combat fighters, tactical and strategic bombers and as interceptors. It is probable that the same evolutionary pressures will result in future UAV's assuming more diverse roles and becoming ever more specialized in their intended purpose.

The US first extensively employed its advanced UAV's during military operations in both Iraq and Afghanistan. They are also currently being utilized as part of its various Shadow War operations occurring over Ukraine and throughout the Middle East and Asia. These systems are predominantly used to provide situational awareness about that which is occurring on the ground and in the sky below the UAV. The acquired data in distributed internally within departments of the US government and military where it might prove useful. It can also be shared with the similar organizations of an ally nation. UAV's are also used to identify high value targets, such as the location of enemy military commanders, ammo depots, missile launch sites, radar units and naval vessels. The UAV operator can then promptly launch a Hellfire missile at the target or provide target attack co-ordinates to other military systems in the area such as strike aircraft or artillery positions. UAV's have also been commonly used by the US in the Middle East and over Afghanistan and Pakistan to hunt down terrorists in hiding, targeting them with Hellfire missiles when and where found. Typically diplomatic arrangements are agreed to in advance to permit American UAV's to neutralize targets hiding within countries with which the US is not at war.

The first advanced American UAV's were the RQ-4 Global Hawk surveillance UAV and the MQ-1 Predator attack UAV. The Global Hawk entered service In 1998 and is a dedicated surveillance platform able to remain in flight for up to 34 hours. The Global Hawk has a length of 47 feet (14 meters), a wingspan of 130 feet (40 meters), an empty weight of 15,000 pounds (6800 kg) and a gross weight of 32,500 pounds (14,600 kg). It is powered by a turbofan engine and operated by a ground crew of three. These include a launch and recovery pilot, a mission pilot, and a sensor operator. The UAV has a cruising speed of 360 mph (570 km/hr), a range of 14,000 miles (23,000 km) and a service ceiling of 66,000 feet (18,000 meters). The RQ-4 is loaded with sophisticated surveillance equipment including a synthetic aperture radar and electro-optical/infrared sensors. Able to perform broad survey's over an area the size of Iceland in a day, the Global Hawk can also zoom in on individual features, providing precision target strike co-ordinates to associated attack platforms.

RQ-4B Global Hawk
Credit: northropgrumman.com

The Predator is an Unmanned Combat Aerial Vehicles (UCAV), capable of both reconnaissance and attack. Entering service in 1995 and powered by a turboprop, it has an operational duration of 14 hours. With its payload of hellfire missiles, the Predator is aptly named. Like an Eagle in the sky, The MQ-1 scans the ground below with precision eyes for opponents who are not even aware that they are being watched. Able to perform its mission day or night, shine or cloud, the Predator can launch instantaneous destruction upon any identified enemy. The first UCAV attack on a ground target occurred in 2001 in Afghanistan when a Predator launched a hellfire into the compound of the leader of the Taliban. Insurgents in Iraq and Afghanistan were soon too scared to leave their houses and too frightened to pick up their cell phones, fearing that they would soon be on the receiving end of a missile flying through their living room window.

MQ-1 Predator
Credit: US Air Force Defense Visual Information Distribution Service

The MQ-1 Predator changed the nature of warfare in both Iraq and Afghanistan. Insurgents in these nations had developed asymmetric warfare tactics that avoided their having to directly confront the full power of the US military, similar as had occurred during the Vietnam War with the hit-and-run tactics employed by the Viet Cong. Relying upon concealed positions and moving under the cover of the night while launching surprise ambushes and aggressive raids, such forces could attack isolated infantry units before armor, artillery or airpower could respond. But the use of UAV's quickly returned the advantage and initiative back to the American forces, providing them with their own asymmetrical warfare capabilities. UCAV's, cruising high above their own troop positions, watched intently for any indications of surprise attacks upon those troops. Ambushing insurgents soon found themselves on the defense, under fire by both the ground troops they were attacking as well as by Hellfire missiles launched by the Predator.

The MQ-1 Predator marked the introduction of a new transformative technology, with its success revolutionizing modern warfare and brining about a worldwide change in tactics and weapons development. Soon other nations were also developing their own arsenals of surveillance, attack and kamikaze UAV's, while the US continued to advance their own UAV technology. The MQ-1 evolved into the even more formidable MQ-9 Reaper. In addition to Hellfire missiles, American UCAV's were also fitted with Stinger air-to-air missiles to provide them an ability to discourage potential aerial assailants. And a new emphasis was placed on the training of personnel to maintain, operate and remotely pilot these new weapon systems. By 2014 the USAF was training more UAV pilots than manned aircraft pilots. More than 20 countries now regularly operate military UAV's and have extensive drone pilot training programs.

Following its introduction in 2007, the MQ-9 Reaper quickly became America's dominant eye-in-the-sky, used extensively to monitor and respond to situations in the ever-volatile Middle East. Most recently the Reaper has been used in this theatre to protect US, Israeli and Saudi Arabian interests from Iranian incursions. Iran has been providing missiles to their allies in Gaza, Lebanon, Syrian and Yemen, who then launch these toward Israeli and Saudi military installations and urban centers. Iran has been spoofing GPS signals to draw oil tankers destined for Saudi Arabia into Iranian waters, at which point they use small craft to board and seize the tankers. Reapers flying overhead can scan large sections of the land and sea below for up to 30 hours at a time over a range of 1,150 miles (1840 km) to track such activities as they occur.

Armed with AGM-114 Hellfire missiles, GBU-12 Paveway II or JDAM's, the Reaper provides substantlal ground and sea attack capabilities as required. The operational costs associated with a Reaper however amount to only about a tenth of that to maintain a fighter aircraft. In 2019 a Reaper was involved in an incident that refined the boundary of declared warfare. Iran tried unsuccessfully to shoot down a Reaper that was investigating an Iranian attack on an oil tanker. If it had been a piloted aircraft that Iran had launched a missile toward, then such an action would have constituted an act of war. The missile launch upon the Reaper, while still being regarded as a militarily offensive action, was not however considered by the United States to constitute an act of war. UAV's therefore provide a useful means to perform military operations that might otherwise have been avoided if a manned system were required to be employed due to the inherent risk of escalation.

A MQ-9 Reaper equipped with a heavy payload of ordnance.
Credit: bellenews.com

Also developed from the MQ-1 Predator is the MQ-1C Gray Eagle, introduced in 2009. A large surveillance UAV, the Gray Eagle replaced earlier RQ-4 Global Hawk's. It has also largely replaced use of the vulnerable manned OH-58D Kiowa Warrior helicopter in this role. The Gray Eagle is much less expensive to operate than a piloted helicopter and can be used to perform recon over dangerous locations without putting personnel at risk. This includes the critical monitoring of North Korean and Iranian nuclear missile development activities. Unlike the Predator which is controlled through a satellite data-link, The Gray Eagle is guided through direct ground control, improving its response time by reducing the time required for signals to be relayed. The Gray Eagle can also be used as a forward long-range eye-in-the-sky by other aircraft. Operated by the crew of a AH-64 Apache helicopter, the MQ-1C can be used to seek out targets that the Apache can then launch remote missile attacks toward. Though a surveillance aircraft, Gray Eagle's can also be equipped with Hellfire or Viper Strike missiles. This capability can be used by the AH-64 crew to have the MQ-1C identify and engage forward threats, clearing a safe path between the Apache and its own primary target. Gray Eagle's also have on-board the equipment required for them to jam enemy radio communications, and so can be used by an advancing Apache attack force to disrupt their opponent's ability to co-ordinate an effective defensive response.

MQ-IC Gray Eagle
Credit: Photo Courtesy of U.S. Army

Where the Predator was used as a baseline to develop the Reaper and the Gray Eagle, the US Navy produced the MQ-4 Triton maritime reconnaissance UAV based on the RQ-4

Global Hawk. The Triton is almost 50 feet (15 meters) long, is over 130 feet (40 meters) across at the wings and is powered by a single turbofan engine that provides it a maximum operating speed of 370 mph (595 km/hr). The UAV is equipped with a radar unit to avoid mid-air collisions and can stay aloft for 24 hours at a time. Cruising at up to 56,000 feet (17,000 meters) and able to fly out to 2700 miles (4340 km) from its launch location, the Triton can survey large areas of ocean as well as focus in on particular points of interest. On-board sensors include electro-optical and infrared cameras designed to spot objects on the ocean and then to zoom in to closely inspect them, as well as low and high band signal receivers that are able to detect both radio and radar transmissions from surface vessels. The Triton can analyze these emissions as well as use them to accurately track the targets. The sensor payload suite aboard the Triton can be modified before launch, enabling its configuration to be selected so that it best meets each specific mission objectives.

A USN MQ-4 Triton maritime reconnaissance UAV
Credit: tvd.im

The premier American UAV is the RQ-170 Sentinel, a stealth flying wing style surveillance UAV with a wingspan of about 90 feet (27 meters). The Sentinel is designed to penetrate a heavily contested state-of-the-art enemy airspace to perform ISR missions and to function as an advanced communications relay node, integrating datalink technologies to transmit precision targeting information to air and ground launch platforms. Introduced in 2007 the Sentinel has seen extensive service flying over Iran and North Korea, investigating nuclear weapons and long-range rocket development programs. With a sophisticated suite of on-board electro-optical and infrared sensors and a very sensitive AESA synthetic aperture radar, the Sentinel can both collect information as well as to function as a precision long-range acquisition and targeting system.

An RQ-170 Sentinel
Credit: worldwarwings.com

One of the highly secretive RQ-170's unfortunately was captured by Iran in 2011. The Iranians were able to down the UAV by hacking into the on-board computer systems to gain control of the UAV. This is a critical example of the susceptibility of sophisticated equipment to acts of cyber warfare, which is discussed in detail in the next chapter. While the US has since introduced upgrades to avoid a similar future incident, this does not reduce the damage done by the loss of the RQ-170.

After examining the UAV themselves, Iranians then handed the RQ-170 over to the Russians. This presumably provided both nations a huge leap forward in their respective UAV technologies. The Russians have subsequently produced the Sukhoi's S-70 Hunter-B, also known as the Okhotnik-B or Hunter-B. The S-70 is an unmanned combat air vehicle that looks unsurprisingly much like the RQ-170. The stealth appearing UCAV is 46 foot (14 meter) long, powered by a turbofan jet and claimed to be able to launch both ground-attack munitions and air-to-air missiles from an internalized bomb bay. The UAV is planned to enter production and initial service in 2024. Of course the strain of the Ukrainian invasion on the Russian military fabrication supply chain system may very well result in delays.

Russia's Sukhoi S-70 Okhotnik UCAV
Credit: militaryleak.com

Other than this one notable example, Russia has otherwise lagged appreciably in the development of UAV's. Having only produced a number of the smaller rail launched versions, Russia has actually had to rely upon purchasing

UAV's from Iran and China to assist them in their invasion of Ukraine. China however has been very active in recent years in developing UAV's, from small surveillance UAV's to large UCAV's. Many of these are based on American UAV designs, with some being flagrant copies. Introduced in 2017, the Chinese TB-001 Scorpion is an effort to produce a UCAV with capabilities similar to the Predator. With a twin tail design and piston engine driven propellers the Scorpion is able to perform long-range intelligence, surveillance, and reconnaissance (ISR). With hardpoints mounted under the wings, the Scorpion can also carry a payload of missiles and bombs. It is 33 feet (10 meters) in length with a wingspan of twice this, a maximum weight of 6000 pounds (2800 kg), a range of 3700 miles (6000 km), service ceiling of 26,000 feet (8000 meters) and an endurance of 35 hours. Scorpion's have been observed frequently flying near both Japan and Taiwan by the authorities of each of these nations.

TB-001 Scorpion
credit Globalsecurity.org

The Chinese have also attempted to produce a long-range high-altitude surveillance aircraft on par with the Global Hawk, known as the WZ-7 Soar Eagle. Entering service in 2018, the Soar Eagle has a wingspan of 80 feet (24 meters) and is thought to have a flight duration of 10 hours. Powered by a turbojet, the Soar Eagle has a range of 4300 miles (7000 km), a flight ceiling of 60,000 feet (18,000 meters) and a cruising speed of 466 mph (750 km/hr). Soar Eagle's have been spotted by US authorities flying above USN ships operating in the South China Sea. The weakness of Chinese UAV's, much like their indigenous fighter aircraft and helicopters, is poor engine design. The Chinese also currently lack satellites for establishing data links with their UAV. While they are in the process of launching additional communication satellites, it will take China some time to build up the personnel and infrastructure required to professionally operate a large UAV force.

A Chinese Soar Eagle
defence-point.gr

The Chinese have also made UCAV's that are based on the Reaper. The CH-4 Rainbow is a surveillance UCAV able to mount various munitions. The CH-4 has been made available for sale by the Chinese on the international market. It has already been purchased by various Middle Eastern nations including Jordan, Egypt, the UAE, Iraq and Saudi Arabia. These nations were also offered UCAV's by the US, but they thought that the American UCAV's were too expensive and came with too many restrictive security conditions attached. China has been selling their equipment at a low cost in an effort to establish themselves as a reputable arms supplier, claiming that their technology is on par with the Americans. Middle Eastern nations however have been scrapping their Chinese UCAV's after a few years of service and replacing them with American counterparts. Apparently the nations that purchase Chinese UAV's are disappointed with their performance. As well Chinese UAV's and UCAV's require constant extensive maintenance and hence are seldom operable. To address this concern the Chinese have upgraded the CH-4 to the more advanced and presumably more reliable CH-5 and CH-6 versions. The WJ-700 is another Chinese manufactured UCAV that has an appearance reminiscent to the Reaper. Expected to enter service in the near future, it is claimed to be able to launch air-to-air missiles, ground attack munitions and anti-shipping missiles.

WJ-700 (left) and CH-4 (right)
Credit: aerotime.aero for WJ-700, pakstrategic.com for CH-4

Israel also became an early leader in UAV development. The main UAV's/UCAV's they produce are known as the Eitan (Heron TP), the Shoval (Heron 1), the Zik (Hermes 450) and the Kohav (Hermes 900). The Eitan is a surveillance UAV that is 49 feet (15 meters) long, has a 30 hour endurance, a service ceiling of 40,000 feet (12,000 meters) and can fly out to 600 miles (1000 km) from its launch point. It is equipped with electro-optical sensors and a satellite data link. The Eitan is optimized for supporting ground troops by performing intelligence gathering missions, identifying opposing targets and tracking their movements. Like many UAV's, it is capable of automated take-off and landing. The Eitan has seen service in multiple conflicts since its inception in 2008. The Shoval is a more modern version of the Eitan, while the Zik is a UCAV with a range of 180 miles (300 km) and an operational endurance of 18 hours. It saw significant use during the 2006 Lebanon War. The Kohav is a long endurance version of Zik that is larger and has expanded capabilities.

The Eitan (left) and Kohav (right)
Credit: dronetechplanet.com (left) and i-hls.com (right)

Turkey has also become a leader in UAV design and manufacturing. Initially procuring Israeli UAV's, Turkey then used the lessons learned from employing these units to focus on developing their own UAV's that were better suited to their own specific requirements. Turkey's best known UCAV is the Bayraktar TB2. At 21 feet (6.4 meters) long, it has an operational duration of 27 hours and an operational ceiling of 25,000 feet (7600 meters). Of a V-tail design and carbon fiber and Kevlar composite construction, the Bayraktar TB2 comes equipped with an electro-optical camera, infrared camera, laser designator and laser range finder. It provides excellent surveillance capabilities at a low unit cost and can be armed with up to four laser-guided missiles. The Turks have used the Bayraktar TB2 to good effect in their conflict with Syria to attack and destroy Russian manufactured and Syrian operated air defense systems, as well as to attack open ground troops.

Turkey sold their UAV's to Azerbaijan, which then used them in their dispute with the Republic of Armenia during the brief 2020 Nagorno-Karabakh War. The war demonstrated to the world that inexpensive UAV's could be used successfully by small poor nations to significantly enhance their overall military's effectiveness. During the war Azerbaijan used the Bayraktar TB2 to locate and destroy Armenian air defense units. They achieved this by flying the UCAV's over Armenian positions to get them to turn on, and thereby reveal the position of, their air defense radars. Azerbaijan was then able to destroy the Armenian air defense sites. This provided Azerbaijan uncontested air superiority, which they then used to destroy the Armenian ground forces. Facilitated by the UAV's, in only six weeks the Armenians were no longer able to defend themselves and agreed to a truce.

Bayraktar TB2 UCAV
Credit: dailysabah.com

Demand for the high quality but inexpensive UAV's produced by Turkey following their successful employment during the Azerbaijan-Armenia conflict resulted in Turkey quickly dominating this emerging sales market. Supplied in large numbers to Ukraine, the Bayraktar TB2 has proven itself highly effective in this theatre of war, thwarting the Russian invasion efforts with regularity. Bayraktar TB2's have been used to good effect in both launching missile strikes toward opposing Russian forces, as well as in identifying and laser designating Russian forces for targeting by other weapon systems such as artillery, Javelin's or aircraft launched guided munitions. The Bayraktar TB2 has been so instrumental in repelling the Russians that it has become a symbol of Ukrainian resistance to the Russian invasion.

The Turks have also recently developed the successor to the Bayraktar's TB2, known as the Akinici, which is Turkish for 'Raider'. Larger and more capable than the Bayraktar's TB2, the Akinici is 39 feet (12 meters) long, 65 feet (20 meters) across at the wings, has a combat ceiling of 40,000 feet (12,000 meters) and a maximum loaded weight of 12,000 pounds (5500 kg) with a 3000 pound (1350 kg) payload capacity. The high-altitude long endurance UCAV is able to perform both air-to-ground attack missions and air-to-air attacks. On-board sensors include AESA radar, electro-optical cameras, infrared cameras, a laser designator and a signals intelligence (SIGINT) system. The first units were delivered to the Turkish Armed Forces in 2021 and the Akinici is being reviewed for purchase by Pakistan, Ukraine and Azerbaijan.

AKINCI, shown armed with MK-82 bombs
Credit: Baykar

The Iranian's have also been active designing and building their own UAV's. An early effort resulted in the Karrar UAV.

The Karrar was created by redesigning and reconfiguring aerial targets provided to Iran by the US in the 1970's. By copying the remote-control system on these aircraft and introducing it into a new airframe based on that of the original drone, the Iranian's were able to produce a simple yet inexpensive remote-controlled UAV. The Karrar is launched from a rail system mounted to a truck. It is claimed to be capable of deploying weapons, including anti-aircraft missiles, small anti-shipping missiles, GPS guided bombs and small cruise missiles. While its capabilities are very limited by modern standards, the Karrar was a convenient platform for the Iranians to become introduced to the design and fabrication of UAV's. Based on their learning experience gained through the Karrar, as well as through captured American UAV's, Iran had quickly excelled in the production of capable UAV's.

Iran's latest UCAV's include the Shahed-191 and the Shahed-129. The Shahed-191 is a relatively simple medium altitude UCAV that entered production in 2012 and is reminiscent in terms of size and functionality to the Predator. With a flight endurance of 24 hours and an operational range of 1050 miles (1700 km), it can only travel to a distance from its control point of 120 miles (200 km) due to the limited range of its data-link connection. Its four hardpoints can mount both Iranian built anti-tank missiles and precision-guided bombs and the Shahed-191 been used by Iran to perform both surveillance and airstrikes as part of their on-going operations in Syria. The Shahed-129, known as the Saegheh, is a small sized copy of American Sentinel captured by Iran. Becoming operational in 2016, the Shahed-129 has a wingspan of around 21 feet (6.5

meters), a cruising speed of 180 mph (300 km/hr), a range of 280 miles (450 km), an endurance of 4.5 hours and a flight ceiling of 25,000 feet (7600 meters). Iran claims that the Shahed-129 is able to launch munitions that are stored within an internal weapons bay. Being operated by Iran over Syria, in 2018 Israel shot down a Saegheh when it approached too close to the Syrian-Israeli border. Reviewing the wreckage, Israeli confirmed that the UCAV configuration was based on the Sentinel and they were surprised by the advanced level of technology incorporated into it. Russia has bought both the Shahed-191 and Shahed-129 from Iran and used them regularly during their invasion of Ukraine.

Truck launched Karrar drones.
Iranian Ministry of Defence

Shahed-191 (left) and the Shahed-129 (right)
Credit: http://globalmilitaryreview.blogspot.com/

Loitering Munitions

Another approach taken by some nations in the design of UAV's was the development of the so-called 'Kamikaze drone'. Also known as a 'suicide drone' or more properly as a 'loitering munition', designers realized that rather than creating a large expensive UCAV to operate as a missile launch platform, they could simply make the UAV itself the missile. Loitering munitions can be thought of as remotely piloted cruise missiles. One of the first kamikaze drones to be built was the Israeli Harop. Designed to function as an anti-radiation loitering munition, the Harop can operate in either manual or fully autonomous modes. Cruising above a battlefield the Harop has radar detecting sensors that are able to discern between friendly and enemy radar. When an enemy radar is detected and the onboard computers evaluate the target as a legitimate and valuable asset, the Harop then descends down upon the target and detonates itself upon impact. If no target is found then the UAV simply returns to its originating airfield and autonomously lands itself. The Harop is about 8 feet (2.5 meters) long and has a wingspan of 10 feet (3 meters).

Israeli Harop Anti-Radiation Loitering Munition
Credit: nationstates.net

Currently there is a wide proliferation of loitering munitions available on the market, produced by many nations. There are Kamikaze drones that are launched from airbases, by aircraft, from armored vehicles and by ground troops. Some are large enough to destroy bunkers and tanks, while others are so small as to be barely detectable visually, acoustically or by radar. These smaller Kamikaze drones are typically employed by ground troops to provide them the ability to immediately respond to a non-line-of-sight (NLOS) threat. Before such UAV's were available, these troops would have to call in an air strike or artillery barrage to address the issue, both delaying their progress and increasing the time that they were exposed to risk. An example of these useful little UAV's is the American Switchblade. Introduced in 2012, it is currently used by the USMC and the US Army, as well as has been provided to Ukrainian forces in large numbers. Carried in a backpack or on a vehicle, the Switchblade is only 2 feet (610 mm) in length, weights 6 pounds (2.7 kg) including carrying case and launcher, has a 10 minute flight duration and can travel out to a distance of 6 miles (10 km) from the launch point. It is referred as the Switchblade as the wings fold in when the UAV is inserted into its carrying tube and swing outward once deployed.

The compact yet highly effective Switchblade
Credit: americangrit.com

Once launched, the operator guides the munition through use of visual and infrared cameras as well as by GPS. Communication to the UAV is through radio signal over a digital data link with secured encryption using a range of frequency bands to avoid jamming or interception. The warhead is essentially a 40 mm grenade and can be triggered on impact or fused to detonate at a specific height and distance from the target. Switchblade can approach its target at up to 100 mph (160 km/hr) either horizontally or in a steep dive. The small electric engine that propels the Switchblade is so quiet that an opponent cannot hear the approaching UAV until it is too late. Switchblade can be used singularly to seek out, identify and destroy a known threat or in conjunction with a standard surveillance UAV which relays the position of an identified target to switchblade equipped ground crews, which then engage those targets.

Many loitering munitions are produced in a series, with different sized UAV's and different warheads available. The Israeli's have developed the Hero series of kamikaze drones. The Hero-120 is a 27 pound (12 kg) UAV dispensed from a multi-canister tube styled launcher. Upon being launched the swing-style wings fold out, similar to the Switchblade. Powered by an electric motor that operates a rear mounted propeller, the loitering munition has about 1 hour of flight time and a range of about 25 miles (40 km). Situational awareness is provided by both electro-optical and infrared sensors. The munition can be used to provide ground troops forward reconnaissance and if a threat is identified then the Hero-120 can be used to directly engage the target with its 10 pound (4.5 kg) warhead. This makes the Hero-120 suitable for both anti-personnel and anti-tank roles. The series also includes the Hero-30 and the Hero-400EC. The small Hero-30 UAV has a 1 pound (0.4 kg) warhead, while the large Hero-400EC has a 90 pound (40 kg) warhead. Each Hero series UAV is equipped with a data link for flight control and infrared and electro-optical cameras for surveillance and target identification. The UAV's have on-board software to assist the operator in detecting suitable targets and the UAV's can be recovered and re-used when not detonated. The Hero-120 has been selected by the USMC to mount on various ground vehicles including their LAV-25's and JLTV's.

Hero-120 kamikaze drone
Credit: navylookout.com

Iran has also developed their own loitering munition, the Shahed-136. A large UAV with an estimated range of 1300 miles (2100 km), the Shahed-136 has been supplied by Iran to the Yemeni's Houthi insurgents, who then used it in attacks against the Yemeni's and Saudi's. In 2019 the Houthi launched a number of Shahed-136's, along with some older generation cruise missiles, at Saudi oil infrastructure. The resulting damage temporarily halved Saudi Arabia's oil production, effecting world oil supplies and pricing. Proliferation of inexpensive Kamikaze drones is a concern to the UN as they provide all nations, as well as insurgents and terrorists, access to low cost precision attack weapons that can be employed anonymously and with zero risk to the operators. Imagine for example if Iraqi insurgents had had suicide drones at their disposal. It is anticipated that the widescale availability of inexpensive kamikaze drones will ultimately result in an overall escalation of the occurrence of low-level conflicts around the world.

Iranian Shahed-136 Kamikaze drone.
Credit: english.iswnews.com

The future of UAV's

In addition to the standard surveillance UAV's, attack UCAV's and Kamikaze drones, there are many other types of UAV's already being produced or are in the process of being developed. One interesting concept is the V-bat UAV. The V-bat is being specifically designed to operate within the cluttered environment of a cityscape to better support urban combat operations. Launched vertically like a quadcopter, the V-bat can operated in this mode to navigate between buildings and to perform close-up inspections. It can also transition to a horizontal profile and operate like an aircraft to increase travel speed and decrease fuel consumption, using a set of wings to provide lift. Such vertically launched but horizontally flying UAV's are also being developed to transport critical supplies to front line units, such as medical supplies and various military gear and tools. The APT 70 is a cargo carrying vertically launched UAV that then transitions to horizontal flight. It can transport up to 70 pounds (32 kg) of cargo out to a distance of 35 miles (56 km).

There is also a demand for very small drones to provide individual soldiers on the ground eyes in the sky. Such 'mini-drones' are similar in size to those that you can buy to fly around in your house or background. The flight control software of the militarized versions however is more sophisticated so that the UAV's have better stability in windy conditions than commercially available mini-drones possess. They also have installed enhanced visual sensors as compared to the simple cameras mounted into commercially available mini-drones. Military grade mini-drones provide ground troops with improved situational awareness by letting them safely see around corners or over the next hill. The Black Hornet 3 is a pocket-sized helicopter styled drone currently in use by US forces that has both a video camera and a thermal imager installed to assist soldiers in identifying concealed threats.

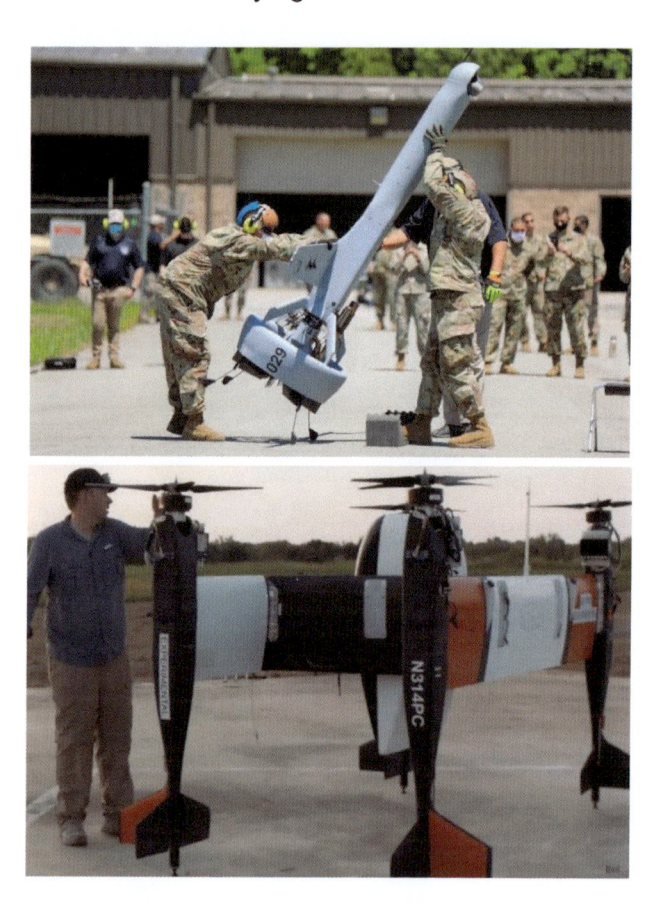

V-BAT UAV (left) and APT-70 (right), each being evaluated by a test team.
Credit: US Army for V-Bat, helis.com for APT-70

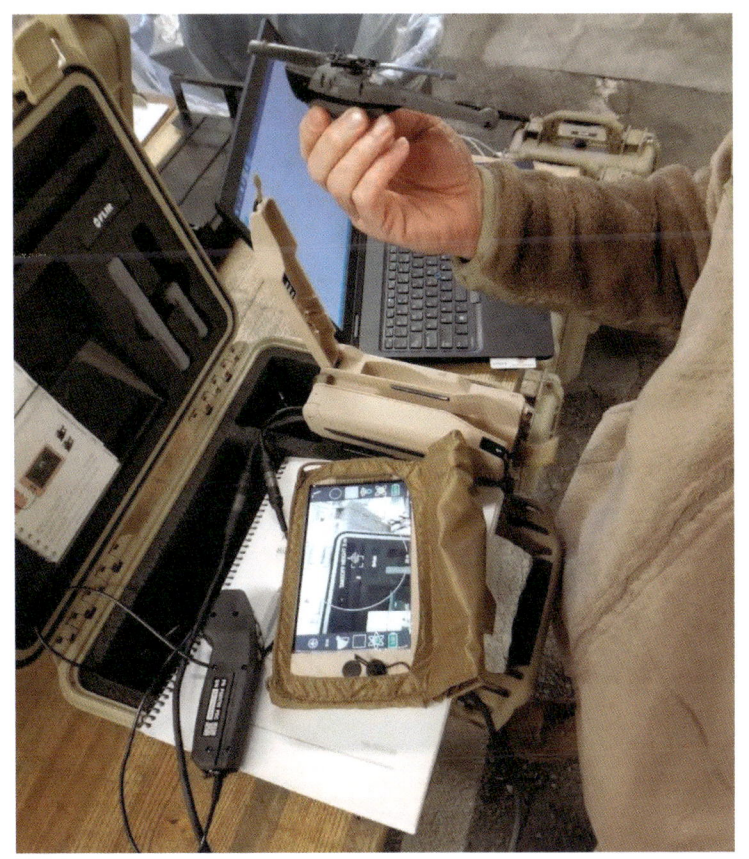

A US Army soldier holds a Black Hornet 3 drone. The other components of the basic package are seen on the table, including the visual control unit.

Credit: US Army

Commercially available UAV's have also found their place on the battlefield without requiring significant modification. During the Russian invasion of Ukraine, the Ukrainians learned to use whatever was at their disposal in their defense. This included deploying large numbers of commercially available UAV's to both survey Russian positions as well as to attack them by dropping munitions from the UAV onto Russian troops and vehicles. In response some manufacturer's, seeing an opportunity to expand their market, began producing more robust versions of their commercial UAV's. They improved the UAV's overall performance as well as increased their resilience to being tracked or shot down. Employment of such simple, inexpensive and generally available UAV's in militarized roles might become a predominant feature of future urban combat, providing ordinary citizens a safe means to participate in the defense of their cities.

An R18 ruggedized octocopter commercial drone. Munitions dropped with the drone are shown beside it.
Credit: Aerorozvidka

Modern UAV's are also having increased levels of autonomy introduced into them. American surveillance UAV's already perform their survey's of the terrain below automatically based on a set of operational instructions. And the Harop can be programmed to fly to a location, loiter in place until on-board software identifies a suitable radar target and then automatically attack the target. Even Iranian built UAV's have an auto-pilot function, allowing them to fly a pre-selected course independently. While Turkey produces the semi-autonomous Songar, an armed quadcopter UAV. Typically transported on a 4x4 vehicle, Songar is deployed when there is suspected enemy activity in the area. The Songar launches and lands itself autonomously, while a pilot operates the UAV during flight to perform target sweeps. The UAV is armed with a stabilized machine gun that carries 200 rounds of 5.56 mm ammunition. Alternatively it can be armed with a 40 mm grenade launcher. The Songar can operate over a radius of 2 miles (3 km) and at an altitude up to 9000 feet (2800 meters). While not stated by the Turkish manufacturer of being capable of full autonomy, it is generally believed that the Songar is enabled to operate in this mode. The UN has made claims that the Songar has been operated fully autonomously against rebel infantry targets in Libya, which if true would be in violation of UN treaties forbidding the use of fully autonomous combat systems in an attack role.

Songar semi-autonomous UAV armed with a machine-gun.
Credit: edrmagazine.eu

Fully autonomous functionality would also provide the opportunity for a UCAV to be employed independently of the operator. This concept has been captured in the concept of the 'Loyal Wingman', an unmanned autonomous UCAV that accompanies a piloted aircraft. The loyal wingman would be configured to be able to perform missions selected by the pilot automatically. A loyal wingman UCAV under development for the USAF is the XQ-58A Valkyrie. The 29 foot (8.8 meter) long jet powered Valkyrie has been undergoing extensive testing and may be ready for deployment within a few years. The Valkyrie is being designed to principally operate as a second set of eyes in the sky, using its extensive sensor suite to detect targets in advance of the manned aircraft. This removes risk to the piloted aircraft, which can remain beyond the detection range of the opponent's air defenses. The piloted aircraft can then safely launch long-range weapons at targets identified by their wingman UAV.

XQ-58A Valkyrie demonstrator.
Credit: USAF

The XQ-58A Valkyrie is also under consideration for the USAF's Skyborg initiative. The goal of Skyborg is to develop and procure a loyal wingman UCAV with sufficient AI capabilities to achieve fully autonomously 'fighter-like performance'. Such a UCAV would be able to perform a broad set of roles including IRS, electronic warfare operations, ground attack missions and engage in aerial combat fully autonomously. The US Navy has also been developing their own prototypes of semi-autonomous UAV's intended to be able to penetrate an opponent's airspace to perform ISR operations, to operate as an aircraft re-fueling program, and as a loyal wingman. Developmental aircraft include the X-47B demonstrator and the MQ-25 Stingray. A great deal was learned from the X-47B project, but it was ultimately cancelled due to high costs. While the Stingray is likely to enter production but will operate in the ISR and re-fueling roles only. Future USAF and USN UAV's are sure to acquire greater autonomy with the ability to perform a greater range of independent functions.

The X-47B (left) and MQ-25 Stingray (right). The Stingray is re-fueling an F-18 in the photo.
Credit: militarymachine.com (left), travelelog.com (right)

Another application under development is that of autonomously functioning swarming loitering munitions.

The concept is that many independently operating Kamikaze drones would be capable of launching a simultaneous coordinated attack on a target. Similar to a massed missile attack, a Kamikaze swarm would be very challenging for an air defense system to defend against because of the number of independent munitions involved. A UAV swarm however offers the additional advantage over a mass missile strike in that the UAV's would be able to actively co-ordinate their attack pattern among themselves. The US, China, Russia and India are each currently researching the development of autonomously controlled UAV swarms. Swarming UAV's are anticipated to be a significant feature of the evolving world of UAV's.

A swarm of 40 test drones being evaluated by the 11th Armored Cavalry Regiment
Credit: U.S. Army Photo by Pv2 James Newsome

The X-61A Gremlin is a USAF swarming UAV program currently under development. Gremlins are launched from an aircraft such as a C-130 from underwing pylons, with up to 8 units being launched and controlled simultaneously. Each Gremlin can be operated fully autonomously or in a semi-autonomous mode, controlled by personnel within the launch aircraft. Gremlin's are designed to work together to provide enhanced capabilities as a networked IRS platform, as an electronic warfare swarm, or to perform synchronized precision kamikaze strikes. Gremlins are pre-loaded with either sensitive surveillance equipment, EW equipment or a HE warhead, with each Gremlin having a payload capacity of 150 pounds (68 kg). Gremlins used in the IRS or EW role are recovered following their mission either in flight through a reeling device or after they land by parachute.

A prototype Gremlin swarming UAV
Credit: flugrevue.de

To counter the quickly evolving roles for UAV's, anti-UAV technologies are being fielded and will constitute a significant factor in future conflicts. Air defense missiles can be launched against large UAV's as they are able to be tracked by radar, are relatively slow moving and not designed to make rapid evasive maneuvers. It is the threat posed by these existing air defense systems that has resulted in newer UAV designs transitioning toward integrating stealth features into their frame structures, similar to the design philosophy being adopted with combat and bomber aircraft. Cyber warfare can also be used to disable or even gain control over an opponent's UAV, as we saw with the Iranian's gaining control over an American Sentinel UAV. This method is particularly effective when the communication link between the remote pilot and the UAV is not secured by encryption or frequency hopping signals.

Addressing penetration of a defensive perimeter by smaller UAV's however is another matter altogether. Air defense missiles are an expensive means to address smaller drones, if they can be successfully used at all in this role. The RCS of small drones is often too insignificant to provide air defense radar systems a target lock. While cyber attacks only have limited success rates and would not be able to deter a swarm of Kamikaze drones. A CIWS can be used to shoot down approaching small UAV's, but these systems are expensive and are generally only installed to protect high value assets such as air bases and naval ships. To counter smaller UAV's the preferred methods are to use Electronic Warfare techniques and directed energy weapons. These can be mounted onto ground vehicles, while some are even compact enough to be used by individual soldiers.

Anti-UAV EW systems generate strong directed radio waves of the frequencies used to operate UAV's with to jam communications between a UAV and its operator. Directed energy weapons by contrast direct powerful high-energy light energy (a laser) or microwave energy (a maser) toward an approaching UAV to destroy sensitive electronics on-board the UAV, to blind it, or to directly destroy it. Both the US and Russia have already developed advanced anti-UAV systems. The Russians employed these systems extensively during their invasion of Ukraine to dissuade the widespread use of UAV's there. The US has also developed a system able to defeat swarming UAV's known as THOR. The system employs a large dish to distribute a broad array of powerfully emitted microwave energy across a large region, disrupting electronics on-board any advancing UAV's.

A 50 kilowatt-class anti-UAV laser integrated with a US Army Stryker vehicle
Credit: US Army

CONCLUSIONS

Military aircraft have experienced significant transformation since their inception in World War I. Modern military aircraft are among the most sophisticated technologies created by humankind. This can likewise be said of the weapon systems which they deploy, and of the weapon systems employed to counter aircraft and to destroy their munitions while in transit to their intended targets. The cost of these aircraft and the systems to counter them are however prohibitive, limiting both the nations that can afford to procure them and the number of systems which can be actively deployed. This has led to an effort to reduce the cost of aerial warfare and has resulted in the development of the relatively inexpensive guided-bomb package and of the unmanned aerial vehicle. Guided munitions permit precision surgical strikes to be performed, while requiring only a small quantity of munitions to be dropped (as compared to the massed carpet bombing campaigns of WWII and Vietnam era warfare). While UAV's permit tasks to be performed by loitering systems that are inexpensive to build and operate, as compared to conventional aircraft, as well as offering the additional advantage of not putting the pilots life at risk. It is not unfathomable to conceive of a world in the relatively near future in which almost all military aerial operations are performed by unmanned automated aircraft, guided under the control of powerful AI programs.

Printed in Great Britain
by Amazon